THE CURIOUS NATURALIST

# Nature's Everyday Mysteries

## A field guide to the world in your backyard

### By Sy Montgomery

WITH A FOREWORD BY
ROGER TORY PETERSON

*Illustrated by Rodica Prato*

CHAPTERS™

CHAPTERS PUBLISHING LTD., SHELBURNE, VERMONT 05482

## Again, to Dr. A.B. Millmoss

Also by Sy Montgomery
*Walking With the Great Apes*

Copyright © 1993 by Sy Montgomery
Illustrations copyright © 1993 by Rodica Prato

Material in this book originally appeared in slightly different form in *The Boston Globe.*

Published by
Chapters Publishing Ltd.
2031 Shelburne Road
Shelburne, Vermont 05482


Library of Congress Cataloguing-in-Publication Data

Montgomery, Sy.
Nature's everyday mysteries : A field guide to the world in your backyard /
by Sy Montgomery.
p.  cm. -- (The Curious naturalist series)
Includes index.
ISBN   0-9631591-9-4  :  $9.95
1. Natural history--Outdoor books.  2. Nature study.  I. Series.
QH81.M83   1993
508--dc20          92-36189
CIP


Trade distribution by
Firefly Books Ltd.
250 Sparks Avenue
Willowdale, Ontario
Canada M2H 2S4

Printed and bound in Canada by
Friesen Printers
Altona, Manitoba

Designed by Hans Teensma/Impress, Inc.

# ACKNOWLEDGMENTS

I AM GRATEFUL to many people who helped create this book. Kathy Everly and Nils Bruzelius, Health and Science editors at *The Boston Globe*, invited me to invent and write the column, "Nature Journal," from which most of these chapters are taken. My thanks for their kind support and thoughtful editing. Also I thank my friend Sandy Taylor, the editor and agent who gathered the columns into this book and matched it to its publisher.

Numerous organizations and institutions opened their archives, provided experts, and shared data to enrich these pages. I acknowledge, in particular, assistance from Cornell University's Laboratory of Ornithology, Harvard University's Department of Entomology, the Massachusetts Division of Fisheries and Wildlife, New England Science Center, the Montshire Museum of Science, Massachusetts Audubon Society, New Hampshire Audubon Society, Antioch/New England Graduate School, and the Harris Center for Conservation Education.

I am indebted to each person quoted in the following pages. I thank them for sharing their knowledge and insights.

Special recognition is due to John Kulish, Eleanor Briggs, Elizabeth Marshall Thomas, Steve Thomas, Ed Duensing, Paul Rezendes, Sue Morse and Judy Garabrant. All served as guides, of sorts, be it through snowdrifts, swamps or Shakespeare. And thanks, also, to Kitty and Jane Bingham for getting me outside at times when even Tess could not.

Finally, I thank Howard Mansfield, my husband. Thanks for your eagle-eyed observations and for being my favorite bipedal walking partner.

# CONTENTS

# FOREWORD

THIS DELIGHTFUL SERIES OF ESSAYS by Sy Montgomery reached me just as I was wearing out from the seemingly endless slavery at my desk and drawing board. In reading them, I could relate to almost every page, every informative chapter, because my home in Connecticut is on 70 acres of second-growth woodland clothing a rocky ridge, with some open spaces, a bit of marshland on the far side and even a man-made pond.

*Nature's Everyday Mysteries* is divided into the four seasons, concentrating on some of the same plant and animal life that I have around my home and that I can observe every day as I walk the long leafy trail from the house to my studio—everything from lowly lichens and fungi to the elitist turkey cocks that act as though they own the place.

This book is a mine of information. It has made me far better informed about the diversity of life around my own home, things that I had taken for granted. Everything from the weather—the mud, rain, ice and snow that wild things must endure; the mammals, such as squirrels, skunks and beavers, and their aerial associates, the birds; down to the ever-abundant flies, mosquitoes and spiders upon which many of them must make their living.

Read Sy Montgomery and enjoy!

*—Roger Tory Peterson*
*Old Lyme, Connecticut*

# INTRODUCTION

W HEN YOU WRITE about nature, you seldom have to
go far for ideas. When I write "Nature Journal"
each month for *The Boston Globe,* from which
most of these chapters were taken, the first step in
my research is often to look out the window.

What I see out of my window is probably similar to what you
see out of yours: the edge of a porch, a stone wall, part of a lawn, a
road, a field bordered by trees, the sky. Yet it's a landscape always
changing: A mushroom appears where there wasn't one yesterday.
A chipmunk races along the stone wall with half his tail missing. A
woolly bear caterpillar crosses the street.

These may seem small details, but they speak of high drama.
The emergence of a mushroom may be the only indication you
will have all year of the life of a creature, neither plant nor animal,
that lives underground and may stretch half a mile long or more.
The chipmunk's missing tail almost invariably testifies not to a
run-in with a predator, as most people assume, but to a turf squabble with another chipmunk. And the woolly bear caterpillar's trip
across the road is, for this tiny animal (the larval form of the tiger
moth), an undertaking as perilous—and as meaningful—as a song-
bird's autumn flight to South America. Both journeys are, in fact,
seasonal migrations.

At this moment, outside your window, in your own backyard,
at your local pond or beach or park, on city streets and sometimes
even inside your house, plants and animals are doing something
incredibly interesting and wholly unexpected. Houseflies are wash-
ing their eyes with their hands and tasting their food with their
feet. Wild turkeys are landing on sidewalks beside parked cars.

Spiders are weaving intricate designs falsely advertising flowers to nectar-eating insects—the silken equivalent of a diner's neon "EATS," which, of course, is what the spider then does. These chapters are intended as a guide to some of these ordinary and astounding events, to suggest new ways to observe and begin to think about the near-at-hand creatures, forces, behaviors and activities that are often overlooked.

Each season, each month offers new natural spectacles, new mysteries to decode. What's that *p-l-oonk* sound coming from the pond? Why does lightning flicker? How do porcupines make love? Why is that rock two different colors? How come North American mosquitoes buzz louder, land harder and itch more than mosquitoes from the tropics? Why don't the frogs in your neighborhood say *ribbit* like the frogs in the movies?

Some months, though, seem less lively than others. Early one New Hampshire March, as I began to cast about for the subject of that month's column, it seemed my window failed me. All I saw out there was mud.

If the window doesn't work, sometimes I walk down to the barn to visit Christopher Hogwood, our pig. (After all, he was the one, along with one of his eight-legged roommates, who gave me the idea for the column on spiders' webs.) So I walked down to see him, but still I wasn't inspired. Everywhere I looked there was only mud.

I thought about going over to my friend's farm in the next town, in case March was less boring over there, but I realized I could never get up her driveway because it had turned into a river of . . . mud.

Then it dawned on me. I phoned my editors at *The Boston Globe* and told them what the subject of my next column would be: Mud.

Mud, it turns out, is full of life. A few years ago, an Ohio biologist removed six square inches of dried-up mud from a dry pasture pool, added water, and three different kinds of tiny animals came out. Estuary mud is even richer: on average, each cubic inch contains 1.4 million microscopic worms and more than a quarter mile of cobweb-thin filaments of fungus known as hyphal threads. There are all different kinds of mud, too—and it helps to be able to tell them apart before one of them swallows up your car.

The book of Job exhorts us to "speak to the earth, and it shall teach thee." Mud, too, has wisdom to impart: to remind us to trust in the richness and generosity of nature, and teach us to expect abundance.

*—Sy Montgomery*
*Hancock, New Hampshire*

# SPRING

# A Porcupine's Private Life

*How the prickly rodents mate,
mingle and maneuver*

**Y**OU'D BE HARD-PRESSED to imagine an animal as unlikely as a porcupine. Its name is Latin for "quill-pig" but actually it's a rodent—a 15-to-30-pound rodent covered with 30,000 three-inch quills. A giant, quilled rodent that can moan, wail, whine, cough, grunt and tooth-chatter and can also dance and swim.

Strangest of all is that the ungainly-looking creature is most often found sitting in a *tree*, of all places—as alarming, it would seem, as looking up to find a beaver perched above us on a branch. Yet there it is, peering down at us, "with a thoughtful, serious look," as naturalist Diana Kappel-Smith writes in her book *Wintering*, "the sober glance of a judge."

Walking through woods near their Athol home, photographer-tracker Paul Rezendes and his naturalist wife, Paulette Roy, saw four porcupines one warm spring day. Too few of us get to see porcupines, perhaps because we don't expect to.

"There are a lot more porcupines out there than people think," says Molly Hale, a University of Massachusetts graduate student who's been studying porcupines at Quabbin Reservoir in Massachusetts. And before trees break into full leaf, your chances of seeing a porcupine couldn't be better.

Most of the year, porcupines sleep in their dens by day, hidden in rock piles and tree hollows, climbing and eating trees after dusk. But during spring, porcupines are often active in broad daylight, especially on mild days when it's warmer outside their dens than in.

"In spring, porcupines are changing their whole regimen," explains Rezendes. Over the winter, they've been eating the bark and needles of hemlock and white pine and the twigs and bark of aspen. To conserve energy, an individual porcupine may eat from only one or two trees all winter. You may see where a porcupine has "flat topped" a favorite tree, giving it the look of a crew cut, or spot a three-to-four-foot-wide band of missing bark where a wintering porcupine has girdled a trunk.

But now, as plants pour nutrients into emerging leaves, porcupines roam more boldly. They may travel over a mile from their dens to sample maple buds, raspberry leaves, the catkins of aspen and the unfurling leaves of beech. They may even visit suburban yards.

The amateur naturalist couldn't ask for a better animal to watch. First, as Rezendes points out, "They're easy to find if you know where to look." You'll discover their dens among ledges and crevices, in boulder fields on the sides of hills and in hemlock trees; another good clue to their whereabouts is mounds of mildly turpentine-scented pellets that look like brown elbow macaroni— porcupine droppings.

Second, you can tell individual porcupines apart by their faces. Author Kappel-Smith finds porcupines' faces "strangely apelike"; others have remarked that certain porcupines have faces exactly like humans'. "What strikes me," says Rezendes, "is porcupines look so different from one another. Sometimes you notice their nose or their dark yellow teeth; some have little tiny eyes, some look very piglike; some are real cute."

And finally, what makes porcupines ideal is that if you don't do anything untoward, they won't run away from you. You can watch them for a long time.

The Czech philosopher Erazim Kohak so loves watching the

porcupines in the woods of his part-time home in New Hampshire that the creatures make several appearances in his 1984 book of philosophy, *The Embers and the Stars.* He has even seen them swim. Their quills are hollow, acting like little life vests.

Rezendes has walked astride a waddling porcupine without the animal so much as raising a quill in annoyance. One day, a porcupine mother and two young "porcupettes" came out of the woods into a field to eat white-clover blossoms and walked right up to where he and Roy were sitting. They crawled up over Rezendes' photography gear; one baby waddled over his wife's toe.

Not only will a porcupine seldom flee, it might not even wake up. Rezendes and Roy went out to photograph a porcupine that lives near their house and found it wouldn't even open its eyes for the occasion. "We yelled at it, we whistled at it, but it just wouldn't wake up," said Rezendes. "They're sleepyheads sometimes."

Or perhaps they are merely serene. There may well be, as the military insists, a certain security that only tens of thousands of potentially lethal weapons can bring. Quills have made porcupines tremendously successful. Besides our North American porcupine, there are 20 other species living all over the world, including porcupines in South America with naked, gripping tails like opossums' and African crested porcupines that sport quills a foot long. India's crested porcupines are similarly armed, and naturalist George Schaller has found 10-foot, 600-pound tigers dead after run-ins with the prickly rodents.

Porcupines don't throw their quills, but they will slap with their tails if provoked. The quills fall out of the porcupine on contact. And then, because the whole shaft of the quill is covered with microscopic barbs, the quills work deeper and deeper into the victim's flesh. A quill can kill if it pierces a vital organ. (If your pet gets quilled, remove the quills promptly. Snip off the hollow tips with scissors to deflate them, then yank them out with pliers.)

Porcupines occasionally quill one another and can even quill themselves. Though adept climbers (with long, curved claws, they scale trees straight up, like a telephone lineman; the stiff bristles on the underside of the tail help prevent backsliding), porcupines do fall out of trees. Uldis Roze, a Queens College professor, examined 15 porcupine skeletons in museums, and nine showed healed fractures. For this reason, says Roze, "porcupines carry a medical insurance policy against their own most formidable weapon": their quills, he says, contain a natural antibiotic.

The notion came to him after a porcupine he was trying to capture drove a quill deep into his upper arm. The quill emerged two days later from his lower forearm, while he was teaching a class. Though it hurt terribly, the wound never became infected. Intrigued, Roze, who trained as a pharmacologist, made an extract of porcupine quills and found it contained a fatty acid that slowed the growth of bacteria.

Still, getting quilled is no fun, so porcupines take care to avoid quilling one another. Molly Hale has found up to five porcupines sharing a single den, and when one enters, she says, you can hear churring and squeaking, probably to alert the others to move over.

Porcupines are equally delicate in romance (their breeding season occurs between September and December). Courtship begins with a dance: both male and female stand on hind legs, touch noses, then drop to all fours and twirl. If the female is impressed, she will back up to the male and hold her dangerous tail aside. Rearing up on his hind legs, the male leans against her, resting lightly on one paw placed against the bristly but quill-free underside of her tail. A little over 200 days later, in late spring or summer, the mother gives birth to a soft-quilled baby.

Porcupines aren't all prickles: "They're rotund, with wonderful bellies, tubby soft bellies," notes Hale. When she live-traps and tranquilizes them to fit them with radio collars, she sometimes strokes them, even their feet. "You know those gardening gloves with the little rubber dots on them? That's what their feet are like," she says. "It helps them climb. Wonderful, wonderful feet."

# Athletics and Ardor

*Courtship in the world of birds*

O N EARLY SPRING evenings, an open field near a low, wet woods provides the stage for a spectacle of athleticism and ardor. The American woodcock, a long-billed, long-legged wader like a sandpiper, normally inhabits upland shores; but at this time of year, at dusk and dawn, the bird seeks out nearby meadows and fields—often even suburban schoolyards.

The male selects a bare spot, a rock or some moss. Positioning himself near center stage, he cocks his tail upward, issues a hiccoughing note and speaks a series of nasal, buzzing *peent*s. Then he begins his spiraling upward flight, curling wider and wider in the sky, twittering as he circles, until the bird is only a speck 300 feet above. And then he falls, literally tumbling from the sky, singing a warbling note. Only feet from the ground, he rights himself and begins the display again. He will repeat it until he attracts a mate.

Spring's mating season brings out birds' showiest displays, their most complex songs, their most dramatic behaviors.

Pairs of red-shouldered hawks, flying with legs extended like landing gear, grab one another's talons in midair. Male woodpeckers begin their early-morning territorial drumrolling on specially chosen resonating trees. Sleek black-and-beige cedar waxwings, easily identified by their jaylike crests, flirt by passing food back and forth: the male, holding a berry in his beak, hops sideways toward the female and passes it to her beak. The female hops away, then toward the male, and passes it back. This food passing may continue for 15 minutes before one of the birds eats the berry.

Early morning and early evening are usually the best times for bird watching. Binoculars are handy, as is a good field guide— Donald and Lillian Stokes' *Bird Behavior* is an excellent one. For the best view, keep the sun at your back so that you can clearly see the bird's color and markings. Another helpful hint: if you know the call of the bird you're watching, speak in the opposite pitch, and it will be less likely to hear you.

This time of year, you need not venture far afield to watch some intimate avian rituals. The common city pigeon exhibits at least six different courtship displays, some of which look quite like dancing. When courting, a male pigeon will ruffle his iridescent neck feathers, lower his head and walk in a distinctive figure eight, alternating with a tail-dragging strut. Once bonded, the couple dance together: the female puts her bill inside her mate's open mouth, and the two move their heads rhythmically up and down.

Mallard ducks, which can be seen near virtually any city park with a pond, indulge in elaborate group displays. Three or more swimming males may perform at once for the benefit of a single female. With shaking heads and tails, arching necks, stretching wings and nodding heads, the males toss droplets of water and emit unducklike whistles to attract a particular female's attention.

Even starlings, those despised European imports (descendants of 40 pairs released in Central Park in 1890 by a New York entrepreneur who wanted to introduce all bird species mentioned in Shakespeare's plays), perform fascinating, uncannily humanlike nesting behavior. Once the male has attracted a female by filling a suitable nest cavity (a tree hollow or cranny of a building) with dead leaves, bark and mosses, the female takes over. She completely clears out everything the male has put into the nest and does it over herself with grasses, while the male perches nearby, watching rather helplessly.

The most obvious and beloved of birds' springtime activities,

TO GAIN THE ATTENTION OF FEMALES,
MALE MALLARD DUCKS ENGAGE IN
ELABORATE COURTSHIP DISPLAYS.

however, is song—an aural advertisement that at once warns and beckons. Many male birds' spring songs are directed first at other males, notes Massachusetts Audubon Society ornithologist Wayne Petersen. Male red-winged blackbirds first *ook-a-leeee* to one another, while spreading their wings to flash and quiver their spectacular red-and-yellow epaulets. The females don't arrive until later. In the early spring, male chickadees answer each other's *fee-bee* whistles, singing their boundaries to one another. Only later, when the birds are in flocks, will groups of both sexes sing out their name, *chickadeedeedeedee.*

Not all birds are this musical. Woodpeckers, for instance, advertise territory and attract females by drumming trees with their beaks—the louder the better. "People call us up when they find their gutter is a particularly attractive drumming area for a woodpecker," said Petersen. "The drumming subsides in a few weeks, but meanwhile, it drives them crazy."

The male ruffed grouse, on the other hand, drums with his wings. This large ground bird lays claim to a thick stand of aspen and attracts a mate by beating his wings to produce a hollow, accelerating drumming. At the same time, he raises his head crest, extends his neck ruff and fans his tail, turkeylike, to its full extent. Only if you are lucky will you see the timid male's display, which is usually performed near sunrise. More often, you will hear it: under favorable wind conditions, the sound can carry more than a mile.

# Nature's Lacework

*The facts, fables and folklore of ferns*

**T**HEY EMERGE from the earth coiled like watch springs. No mere straight green shoots for the plant that matures into what author and botanist William Nelson Clute called "nature's lacework." No, the spring-woken fern, unique among all buds, is a spiral. And in early spring, these shapes can be seen everywhere.

The silvery white heads of cinnamon ferns peep up from bogs; the Christmas fern's backward-leaning buds rise from rocky hillsides; the croquet hoops of newly emerging bracken ferns grace open spaces.

Resembling the scroll of a violin, these spiraled buds are named fiddleheads. Some may grow an inch a day. Their fronds seem to burst from the earth with an energy we normally accord only to animals: one writer sees them "curling and twisting like dancers"; another describes them "uncoiling like tiny green serpents."

No wonder ferns evoke such poetic imagery. Beautiful, ancient and mysterious, ferns reawaken us each spring to the world of the dinosaurs and reenchant us with the magic of fable and legend.

Eons before the first bees, flowers or fruits, ferns grew in luxuriance from the equator to the poles. Many towered 50 feet tall, with woody trunks and six-foot leaves. Today, there still are forests of ferns in places like New Zealand and Hawaii. (In fact, Austria's best-known living artist, Friendensreich Hundertwasser, redesigned the national flag of New Zealand to feature a stylized fiddlehead, but New Zealand turned it down.) Ferns dominated the dinosaurs' green world, along with liverworts, mosses and lichens.

Ferns still reproduce in the ancient way, without flowers or seed. This fact confounded botanists for centuries. Such an inexplicably unplantlike trait could be attributed only to divine indignation. At the birth of Jesus, one Old World legend goes, all the other plants in the straw cradling the Christ Child put forth flowers; but the ferns forgot to bloom and have been denied flowers ever since.

Other beliefs held that ferns *did* flower and set seed, but the event was so rare and so brief that most people missed it. The flowers were said to be tiny and blue and the luminous seeds yet smaller. Fern seed possessed magical powers: throughout Medieval Europe, on Midsummer's Eve, people foraged in the forest with white cloths in hand to catch the magical fern seed when it ripened at the stroke of midnight. "We have the receipt for fernseed," Gadshill announces in Shakespeare's *Henry IV*—and jubilantly he proclaims the result: "We walk invisible."

Invisibility was only one of the powers fern seed could bestow. A Russian legend held that fern seed conferred second sight: As a cattle herder searched for his animals, fern seed fell into his shoes, and immediately, he knew not only where his cattle were, but also the location of buried treasure. He went home for a shovel to dig it up, but unfortunately changed shoes and completely lost the insight.

When microscopes were invented, botanists hoped that they might glimpse the fabled fern seed at last. But what they found under their microscopes were not seeds but something even more magical: dustlike dots so light they cross oceans on the wind; tiny specks that contain within them plans for creatures totally unlike their parent.

The plant that grows from a fern spore looks as different from a fern as a lily pad from an oak. Carried far from its parent by the wind, the spore grows into a tiny heart-shaped plant as small as a child's fingernail. This creature, called a prothallium, is a hermaphrodite. From the union of its own egg and sperm, it produces a third generation—this time, one that will look like its grandparent. The prothallium lives only a few months, but its offspring may live for a hundred years; within four to seven years, the new fern will produce spores of its own.

If you turn over the leaves of a mature fern in the summer, you may see where the spores are stored. Some ferns bear spores on special fronds called fertile spikes, but most arrange their spores in little packages called sori. You can often identify different species of ferns this way: the marginal wood fern's sori are on the edge of the underside of the leaf, and they look like curled-up caterpillars. The sori of the leathery-leaved polypody fern resemble freckles. When a fern releases its spores in the summer, you can sometimes hear the sori snap open—but trying to be there for that event may prove as difficult as capturing fern seed on Midsummer's Eve.

Folks still comb the woods and fields for ferns, but these days, it is for magic of a culinary nature. Cooked like asparagus, the young fiddleheads of bracken, cinnamon and ostrich ferns are considered delicacies. Because some supermarkets sell them simply as "fiddleheads"—which is only the word for the coiled fern bud, not the name of a particular species of fern—some people think all fiddleheads are this tasty. Don't make the mistake of cooking up the wrong ferns. Many people have done this, usually with the fiddleheads of the interrupted fern, which have a white woollike covering. The result is a dish with all the taste appeal of green hairballs.

But now there's a caveat to even the edible fiddleheads: at least one kind of bracken fern contains toxins that, when USDA scientists fed them to laboratory rats, caused intestinal cancer. Because of that data, some wild-foods aficionados avoid all fiddleheads. Even Ty Minton—a botanist whose first thought at seeing Hawaii's tree ferns was how a single fiddlehead would fill a casserole dish— says he has "backed off" from eating ferns. But Minton also points out that many healthful foods, including cancer-fighting broccoli, contain tiny amounts of natural toxins capable of causing cancer.

In the Old World, toothache was a greater threat than cancer, and here, ferns came to the rescue. Biting a fiddlehead each spring was supposed to ensure against the ailment for a full year. Ferns also helped people manipulate the weather and tell the future. Bracken ferns, when burned, caused rain. In *The Story of Mosses, Ferns and Mushrooms,* author Dorothy Sterling writes that an early English king forbade the burning of bracken during his visit to Staffordshire. Sure enough, his vacation was sunny. Bracken also protected against goblins and witches and would foretell the initial of your future spouse in its cut stem. (This definitely works—if your intended's name begins with the letter C.)

Whether or not ferns can bestow special powers, it never hurts to stuff a fern in your shoe. It may not lead you to buried treasure, but the soft foliage will help cushion your feet if they are sore from your walk in the woods.

# Croak of the Wild

*Frogs' mating rituals*

TO EARN his master's degree, Bryan Windmiller, a graduate biology student at Tufts University, spent his spring mornings and many of his evenings counting frogs. For this purpose, he placed 62 five-gallon buckets around a shallow pond in Concord, Massachusetts.

One morning, he counted 360 wood frogs and 211 spring peepers, not to mention 33 spotted salamanders and two blue-spotted salamanders. "I was almost up to my elbows in solid amphibians," he said with satisfaction. "It was like some kind of Indiana Jones movie."

The poet T.S. Eliot thought April was the cruelest month; had he been a naturalist working in the northern parts of the United States, he would have pointed out instead that it is the froggiest. April is the time that many of North America's frog species emerge from hibernating under leaf litter and on pond bottoms to do what frogs do best—which is, in the words of author and naturalist Archie Carr, "get together in wet places on warm nights and sing about sex."

The frog voices you hear on spring nights belong to males. Floating in pools, clinging to cattails, even perching on tree trunks, they croak, whir and trill to the females to come join them in the water. Males create their calls by inflating air sacs, which may be located under their chins, on their cheeks or even under their armpits.

If you're not used to frog song, its sudden eruption can be disorienting. About this time of year a few years back, a woman

IN APRIL, FROGS DO WHAT THEY DO BEST:
GET TOGETHER IN WET PLACES ON
WARM NIGHTS AND SING.

called the New England Science Center's zoo, alarmed that a "bizarre animal" was "screaming" outside her window. She sent in a 25-minute tape recording of the mystery animal's voice. Zookeeper Don Winans identified it immediately: the loud, resonating trill, similar to the distress cry of a baby raccoon, belonged to a two-inch-long gray tree frog.

City dwellers experiencing spring in frog country may think aliens have landed when they hear the spring peeper's high-pitched, ascending whistle. A chorus of these little tan tree frogs (sounding, as one field guide describes delightfully, "like the jingle of bells") can carry a mile or more. In some suburban areas, motorists commuting home past ponds and swamps report that even with the car windows rolled up and the stereo playing, they can hear the peepers.

Each frog species has a distinctive voice. Wood frogs—pretty little brown amphibians with black robbers' masks—quack like ducks. Spotted leopard frogs emit throaty croaks. American toads trill musically. Bullfrogs call *jug-o-rum*. The song of the green frog sounds like the twang of a loose banjo string, while the pickerel frog, above water, has a steady, low croak; if the pickerel is underwater, the call sounds like a rolling snore. (Incidentally, most frogs do *not* say *ribbit*; however, a species found near Hollywood, the California tree frog, does—which is why *ribbit* is the line frogs most frequently get to say in the movies.)

If you follow these voices, they'll lead you to frogs—and to scenes that rival X-rated movies. "The breeding strategies of some frogs could really be called orgies," says Tom French, who's watched and collected frogs from Maine to Louisiana.

Wood frogs and American toads, for example, gather in temporary pools to mate in free-for-alls: Floating males grab almost anything that goes by. Several males may latch on to one female, holding on to parts of her body with their forefeet, gripping her tightly by locking their thumbs together, while at the same time kicking at rival males with their back legs, trying to push competitors away. Many females drown from such attentions.

Males often jump atop and grab other males by mistake; some, like American toads, will even embrace surprised salamanders. Male frogs mount other males so frequently that they have a special "release call" to remedy such mistakes. (If you pick up a male toad, he may issue the same special trill he uses for occasions of mistaken identity.)

Other frog species have a different breeding strategy. Each male bullfrog, for example, occupies a territory—a few feet of shallow water at the edge of a permanent pond, usually featuring a nice spot for attaching the female's egg mass—which he will vigorously defend.

Males battle one another by wrestling. They'll stand on their hind legs, pushing themselves out of the shallows as they grab at rivals with their forefeet. Wrestling bouts can go on for a minute or more.

The best time to watch frogs is on a warmish evening, especially when it is raining. Take a flashlight, and cover the light with red cellophane; the frogs won't mind it at all, for they can't see red. Follow the frog song to the nearest body of water, but don't be discouraged if the frogs hush or hide as you approach. You can get them to start up again with a soft, high whistle or by rubbing two stones together. They mistake these sounds for calls of a rival male.

On spring evenings, you're likely to encounter several species sharing a pond. But in your excitement, don't make the mistake scientist Tom French did during a recent frog census. With a gray tree frog in his right hand and a flashlight in his left, he spotted a leopard frog he wanted to catch. "The only place to put the gray tree frog," he explained, "was in my mouth." Unfortunately, as French quickly discovered, the skin of the gray tree frog exudes a foul-tasting, burning substance. It tastes, he said, "like a skunk spraying in your mouth."

# Mud-Luscious

*When the world turns to muck*

THIS IS THE TIME of year when people who live at the end of long dirt driveways get lonely. They don't go out, and nobody, not even the UPS driver, attempts to visit them. The reason, of course, is it's Mud Season, when meltwater and rain can't drain through the soil, and dirt roads and driveways dissolve into car-sinking glop.

Mud is nature at its most unappreciated. Farmers don't like it. Road agents don't like it. Mothers don't like it. And other than e.e. cummings, who called early spring a time "when the world is mud-luscious," most poets don't seem to like it either. (In poetry, there's a lot of dust, but little mud.) Among some circles, in fact, it seems mud is a dirty word.

"I hardly ever use the term," says Jerry Rosenberg, a scientist with the USDA Soil Conservation Service. So what does he call the stuff? "It's soil, with a water content—supersaturated soil." (But Rosenberg doesn't want to blame mud on soil, mind you. "The villain," he points out, in eager defense of soil science, "is the water, not the good old soil." A hydrologist, on the other hand, argues instead that mud results when good old water gets dirtied by nasty soil.)

Linny Donaldson Levin, a naturalist-educator at the Mont-shire Museum in Norwich, Vermont, doesn't like the word "mud" either. "Mud is a real derogatory term for something as important as soil and water," she says. "After all, it's alive."

To prove her point, she describes a 1944 experiment by one

Dr. Ralph W. Dexter: On November 3, the biologist removed six square inches of dried-up mud from a dry pasture pool in northeastern Ohio. To simulate what would happen in spring, he added water to his mud sample.

He didn't have to wait long for results. Within three days, using a microscope, he could detect copepods, nearly transparent crustaceans smaller than a grain of rice, swimming in the muddy water. The following day, the little creatures had bred and were carrying egg sacs on their backs. A month later, a dragonfly larva hatched out of the mud. Two months later, he found strange animals whose front ends were equipped with retractable disks, fringed with hairs that beat in a circular motion. (When they moved, the disks looked like revolving wheels; that's why these animals are called rotifers.) The following month, leeches appeared.

Dexter dubbed his experiment "A Demonstration of Suspended Animation: Sleeping Beauties Come to Life." The parents of these little invertebrates had laid drought-resistant eggs in the drying mud of summer, little time capsules synchronized to hatch when the world again became "mud-luscious" in spring.

Some muds are livelier than others. Driveway and road mud is relatively impoverished, biologically speaking, for the weight of passing cars compacts the grains of soil, blocking the passage of nutrients. (Normal soil is about 50 percent "voids," or space, but driving repeatedly on mud can compact the soil to just 10 percent voids, as agricultural engineering researchers at Ohio State found out.)

Other muds, though they look barren, are seething with life. Estuary mud—found in low salt marshes and mud flats—may sport little visible vegetation; but the mud itself "is loaded with all kinds of goodies," says Rick Van de Poll, an Antioch/New England Graduate School botanist who has been known to wade purposely in mud up to his lips.

Each cubic inch of estuary mud contains, on average, 1.4 million microscopic worms called nematodes and more than one-quarter mile of cobweb-thin filaments of fungus known as hyphal threads. These tiny creatures provide food for other animals, from snails and clams to mud fiddler crabs. In one square foot of estuary mud, you can count as many as 100 air holes made by these shelled creatures.

Such mud, says Van de Poll, operates like "a mini-Gaia system": The organisms that live in the mud re-create and regulate their own environment. In the mud of the salt marsh, for instance, ribbed mussels feed on and live in peat mats. The mussels' excrement, which forms part of the mud, is high in nitrogen, which feeds the salt marsh's cord grass. As the cord grass dies, it forms the peat mats in which the mussels live.

Mud, in its infinite variety, is an integral part of the natural world—yet, while bookstores are stocked with field guides to animal tracks, seashells and stars, there is not yet any popular field guide to mud. To fill that void, here's a primer on some of the more interesting muds you're likely to encounter:

**Clay Mud:** This is the stickiest, gooiest mud, the best for mud pies, pottery-making and mud-wrestling. That's because, of the three major soil types (clay, silt and sand), clay's particles are the finest—$\frac{1}{256}$ of a millimeter in diameter or smaller. When the tiny spaces between these extra-small particles fill up with water, the clay becomes unstable and sticky—or, as John McDowell, chairman of the department of geology at Tulane University, puts it in scientific terms, "It goes gush."

**Muck:** It looks like black mud, but it's not. Mud, technically speaking, is made of finely ground rocks and minerals mixed with water; muck contains up to one-third rotting organic material. Rub muck between your fingers, and you'll feel fibers. Driving in this is a great way to sink your car out of sight.

**Peat:** Peat, on the other hand, contains greater than 66 percent fibers. There are variations, of course, including mucky peat and peaty muck, but these distinctions are for the advanced mudologist.

**Ocean Mud:** You don't have to be a deep-sea diver to find marine mud. You can find mud from the ocean 200 miles inland.

Much of it is buried by inland sand, but you might come across it while you're digging a hole.

**Varves:** Are you living on an old lake bottom? The answer can be found in ancient mud. Lake-bottom muds are two-layered: each winter, as the lake ices over, clay settles out of the water; then each summer, rivers feed the lake with silt and sand. This creates paired mud layers called varves. Count the varves to compute the number of years the land was a lake bottom.

**Armored Mudballs:** Richard Little, a professor of geology at Greenfield (Massachusetts) Community College, was looking at the foundation of a torn-down suspension bridge when he made a surprising geological find. Embedded in cut blocks of conglomerate rock, he saw, in cross section, baseball-sized, reddish brown, pebble-encrusted balls. He had discovered armored mudballs, known from only nine other sites in the world. The armored mudballs formed about 200 million years ago when pieces of mud dropped off the edge of a Mesozoic stream, then rolled into the pebbles of the streambed. The pebbles coated the mud like walnuts on a cheese ball. All the other known armored mudballs come from ocean mud; these are the only stream-formed armored mudballs known in the world.

This fossilized mud can satisfy your mud cravings during times when there is no fresh mud around, for the world is only "mud-luscious" for a short time. Meanwhile, enjoy mud season. And remember to wipe your feet.

# Eating Wild
*Edible roots, weeds and flowers*

A MONDAY-MORNING fantasy we've probably all shared at some time or other is to escape to the South Seas. No need to work; just live off the land, plucking coconuts, pineapples and breadfruit.

Euell Gibbons did it. "I have tried the lotus-eating life of a Pacific beachcomber," the late author and forager wrote, "and found it lacking. I'm sure it will surprise many when I assert that it is easier to 'go native' in many sections of the United States than in the South Seas."

In the spring of the year, for variety, nutrition and taste, the average ungardened backyard provides more good food than the lushest tropical island. Some of the best-tasting wild foods are probably growing on your lawn.

On a vacant lot in Chicago, Gibbons found 15 edible plant species; bordering a single suburban Philadelphia pond, he found 18. Venture just a bit farther afield, say, to the edge of a meadow or wetland, and your menu expands dramatically. Within an hour's walk of any suburban or rural area of the eastern United States, a skilled forager can point out 60 edible plant species. From these, you can prepare salads, casseroles, breads, drinks, condiments, pickles, jams, jellies and preserves.

These are not just foods to keep you from starving. As Easterners battle common lawn weeds like dandelions, sheep sorrel and pigweed, health-food restaurants in California are serving them to well-heeled patrons.

Wild foods—nurtured by rainwater, untouched by most of the pesticides that taint many grocery items, yet far richer in vitamins—are gourmet fare. "Say you have everything in the world," offers Milada Harlow, a naturalist and forager in Lyme, New Hampshire, "but have you ever tasted a tossed wild salad? People really should experience this."

Harlow's particular specialty is edible flowers. Flowers often taste as good as they smell; they are high in vitamins (roses, she says, contain more vitamin C than anything else on Earth); and they look as good on your plate as they do in a vase. At wild-foods seminars, she is eager to tell others about "flowers you really should be eating."

Among them are violets—delightful on open-faced cream-cheese sandwiches or tossed (both flowers and leaves) into salads; roses—the red petals sprinkled on vichyssoise are "out of this world, not only in taste but also appearance"; daylily blossoms and buds—stuff them with cottage cheese mixed with herbs or with crabmeat, tuna or egg salad.

Cultivated flowers, she points out, taste wonderful too. Pluck the flowerlets of lilacs and toss them into salads. Add rose petals for even more stunning color. Gladioli can be stuffed like daylilies. And the big hybrid pansies look beautiful on open-faced sandwiches.

These common flowers are easy to identify, but some plants are more tricky. The tasty, large shoots of skunk cabbage resemble deadly Indian poke, and both grow in wet places. Some plants taste great if they're picked at the right time and prepared in the right way but can be toxic—or taste as if they are—when not prepared or harvested properly. Milkweed shoots, for instance, are mild and delicate if boiled three times, each time in fresh water; otherwise, they can make you sick enough to need days in the hospital. The white roots of burdock, a sturdy plant that looks like a thistle, are edible—but only in the plant's first year. Try the roots of a two-year-old plant, and they'll taste like baling twine.

Ty Minton, a botanist who co-chairs the environmental studies department at Antioch/New England Graduate School in Keene, New Hampshire, stresses safety first: Do not collect edible wild foods along well-traveled roads or near orchards; they may be tainted with pesticides. Confirm that what you're collecting is what you think it is. For guidance, collect with an experienced forager. Or consult a good guide, such as the *Peterson Field Guide to Wild Edible Plants* or Gibbons' *Stalking the Wild Asparagus.* (The Gibbons book also contains recipes for teas, preserves, wines and medicines.)

But you don't need a field guide to identify one of the most delicious wild foods, one that's right on your lawn: the common dandelion.

"Dandelions are just unbelievable," says Rick Van de Poll, an Antioch/New England botanist. "They have more purposes and values than almost anything out there."

From this despised weed, you can make vitamin-A-rich fritters, tempura, salads, cooked greens, desserts, wine and a fine coffee substitute. Start with the dandelion's flowers: Separate the yellow petals from the green petiole, and add them to rhubarb pie or to tossed green salads for color and vitamins. Or leave the petiole on the flower, and dip each blossom in tempura batter or pancake batter. Deep-fry them for a treat similar to fried clams. Many old cookbooks have a recipe for dandelion wine, which is made from the blossoms; there is an excellent one in Gibbons' book.

The tiniest young leaves can be added raw to salads. Cooked (boil once for five minutes; drain the water, and boil in fresh water again, or they will be bitter), the leaves look like spinach but have a taste all their own. Add salt, pepper and butter or margarine.

On top of the dandelion root, you'll find a crown of blanched leaf stems that many consider the plant's tastiest offering. This can be eaten raw, after soaking in cold salted water, or cooked with onions, a pinch of sugar, salt and pepper.

The plant's white root, which gardeners know can grow as fat around as a finger, has at least two uses. For a cooked vegetable, which Gibbons described as tastier than a parsnip, peel a batch of

roots with a potato peeler, and slice them thinly crosswise. Boil
with a pinch of baking soda for five minutes, pour off that water
(again, this removes any bitterness), and boil again until they are
tender.

For an excellent and inexpensive coffee substitute, roast the
raw roots slowly (for about four hours, so do it in a wood stove or
while something else is cooking) until they're brown and brittle.
Then grind them, and use like coffee.

Not bad for a weed. But then again, as Emerson wrote in an
1878 essay, "a weed is a plant whose virtues have simply not been
discovered."

# SUMMER

# Messages in Spiders' Webs

## How false advertising pays off

I N MANY WAYS, the children's classic *Charlotte's Web* is an excellent primer on spider behavior. But, alas, arachnologists (the technical name for researchers who study spiders) tell us not everything in the book is true.

Charlotte, says spider specialist Bill Piel, a graduate student at Harvard, couldn't really have woven the words "SOME PIG" into her web.

Charlotte's last name, he points out, was *A. cavaticus*—"and the real *A. cavaticus* does not weave patterns into its web. Even if it could write, it wouldn't do it in its web. But," he adds quickly, "a garden spider might."

Garden spiders, a Yale researcher has discovered, weave into their webs decorations that, seen in ultraviolet light, look like flowers to nectar-hungry insects. Ultraviolet light is beyond the spectrum of light people can see, but insects can see it. To us, the spiders' designs just look like zigzags, crosses and bars. But to nectar-eating bugs, the designs mimic the ultraviolet light patterns of flowers such as daisies and marigolds—only bigger and bolder, promising a mother lode of food.

Rather than advertising "SOME PIG," the garden spider advertises "EATS"—which, of course, once an insect arrives, the spider does.

Catherine Craig made this discovery while watching giant garden spiders at the Smithsonian Tropical Research Institute in Panama. North American garden spiders—the fat-bodied, black-and-gold spiders who hang center-web in gardens and on bushes—also do this, Craig assures us. "Go out in the early morning, before the sun's up, with a flashlight, when they're building zigzags into their webs," she urges. "They're fascinating to watch."

Spiders offer us a close-up look at some of nature's most dramatic moments. In summer, without leaving your yard—in many cases, without leaving your house—you can watch a typical spider build a web, catch, paralyze, wrap and eat its prey, repair and clean its web and then dismantle much of the structure—all in a 24-hour period.

You will have no trouble finding a spider to observe. Scientists have named about 37,000 spider species in the world so far, which they estimate represents only one-quarter of the actual total. Spiders' webs are everywhere: sheetlike webs in grass, beautiful orbs in windows, funnels in barn corners and mesh around toilet pipes.

Some spiders don't build webs at all, but those that do exhibit a talent unrivaled by any vertebrate. Unlike a beaver's dam or a bird's nest, the spider's web is created from materials made in its own body—a liquid protein changed to solid silk by the very process of pulling it out of its body with its back legs.

The most beautiful of the webs, to human sensibilities, is the classic orb shape: spokes of a wheel overlaid with a spiral. Working with all eight legs, watching with all its eight eyes and spinning with all six spinnerets, a spider can create this marvelous structure in under an hour.

The best times to watch spiders weaving, advises Harvard arachnologist Dr. Herbert Levi, are early morning and early evening. The intricacies of the web will be easier to see if it is between you and the sun. (Levi's other spider-watching advice: "Don't keep the house too clean.")

On orb webs, look carefully at the spiral, which is the snare it-

GARDEN SPIDERS WEAVE PATTERNS IN
THEIR WEBS THAT LOOK LIKE FLOWERS TO
NECTAR-HUNGRY INSECTS.

self: some orb weavers lay down drops of glue here, which are visible with a magnifying glass; others make a kind of natural Velcro by combing and fluffing the silk strand with their back legs so that it tangles and grabs the hairs and legs of insects. The spider doesn't get stuck in its own web because it has oils on its feet, and it stays on the nonsticky part. Spiders eat the sticky strands (like recycling used flypaper) and remake them each day.

Webs are not always passive traps. As Catherine Craig's work shows, a web may be an active lure. She found that garden spiders use a special silk, one that shows up particularly well in ultraviolet light, to make their decorations stand out against the rest of the web. In experiments comparing decorated portions of webs with portions from which the decorations had been removed, Craig discovered that the decorated parts attracted 58 percent more insects per hour.

Other kinds of spiders use their webs as weapons. One species, which commonly builds webs over streams, pulls up its orb into a taut cone and snaps it shut to catch feeble flies. The so-called spitting spider—a yellow-and-black-spotted animal with a large, humped head—shoots a strand of glue mixed with venom at its victim. When you find the sucked-dry husk of a fly stuck to the ceiling, you can be sure a spitting spider enjoyed a meal.

Webs serve yet more unlikely functions. A male spider produces sperm in his abdomen but cannot deposit it in a female until he has spread the sperm onto a special web he builds for the occasion. He then sucks the sperm up into tubes inside two armlike appendages on his head, called pedipalps, and these are the organs with which he inseminates the female.

One reason some people find spiders unappealing is that their body parts seem too numerous and in the wrong places. Their heads are covered with eyes, fangs and legs. To make things even stranger, the spider's sucking stomach is located in its head, not its abdomen (which is the only other body part the spider has).

"A spider's face is pretty awful until you get fond of it," wrote Winifred Duncan, a Cape Cod lady who studied spiders in New

England and abroad in the 1940s. (She became so fond of them, in fact, that she took to capturing spiders in jars and then letting them loose in her house so that she could more readily watch their activities. Her charming book, *Webs in the Wind*, features many drawings of webs the spiders then wove in her bedroom curtains, between chair and hatrack, table and lamp.)

Perhaps the least gruesome spider faces belong to the jumping spiders. "They're the cutest spiders," asserts Bill Piel, a student in Herbert Levi's spider lab. Jumping spiders, of which there are several species, have two big button eyes ("like the headlights on a car," Levi says) and six smaller ones. They stalk their prey visually, jumping like a cat on flies, beetles and moths, leaving a dragline of silk behind. What makes them so appealing, says Piel, is that unlike most other spiders that seem oblivious to your presence, these spiders will look right at you: "A movement of your arm or hand will cause it to focus on you. It's like a squirrel."

The jumping spiders' courtship is heartwarming. The tiny male dances before the larger female, waving legs at her balletically. The dance can go on for 10 minutes before the two mate. Because of the size difference between the two sexes, male spiders are sometimes eaten by their brides. But the long-jawed orb weaver has worked out this solution to the dilemma: when male meets female, he grabs her jaws with his own, and with his fangs, he locks her fangs in the open position—like a kiss. Or like Tarzan propping open the jaws of a crocodile with a stick, whichever way you want to look at it.

# Never Sleep With a Skunk

*And other precautionary tales*

I TS LATIN NAME, *Mephitis,* is synonymous with "stink"—"a noxious, pestilential or foul exhalation from the earth." In the early days of North American exploration, historian Gabriel Sagard-Theodat called it *l'enfant du diable*: child of the devil.

All this simply because the skunk, a handsome, cat-sized relative of the otter, would rather douse you with a stream of oily, amber-colored, gaggingly foul-smelling musk than just stand there and get killed.

Musk is not unique to skunks. A variety of mammals, ranging from certain deer to civets and ferrets, use such glandular secretions to communicate with scent. The skunk's message, however, is perhaps the loudest and clearest. With its body contorted into a U shape, with both head and rear end facing its attacker, a skunk can spray its musk up to 23 feet with the help of a favorable wind; experts report a skunk can hit your face with accuracy at 9 feet. The musk is released from two nozzlelike nipples on either side of the skunk's anus. It can fire either an atomized spray or a stream of rain-sized drops, whichever the skunk deems appropriate.

But skunks actually spray very rarely, and then only as a last resort after other ample warnings have failed. One species, the spotted skunk, not only will stamp loudly and repeatedly and hiss, as do other skunks, but will even perform a handstand before it releases its musk. It is only because cars (and uninformed dogs) pay little attention to such admonitions that our summers are so often perfumed with the skunk's sulfurous smell.

If anything, skunks deserve a reputation for their gracious sense of restraint. Farmers have chased them out of henhouses (they steal eggs) without getting sprayed. Skunks tolerate with aplomb transport in live-traps. A New York researcher who tried to take a mouse away from the young skunk that was eating it wasn't sprayed—though the skunk growled and clung to its rightful prey even as the scientist lifted it a foot off the ground. American Museum of Natural History mammalogist Richard Van Gelder teaches other experts how to pick up wild skunks *by their tails* without getting sprayed. (Warning: Don't try this at home!)

Some people even enjoy the aroma of skunk musk and have a support group of their own, The Whiffy Club, composed entirely of people who *like* the smell of skunk spray. Some Whiffers so relish the aroma that they keep a vial of the scent handy for an invigorating sniff. (That way, "you don't have to wait for one to die," says "Marilyn," the anonymous antiques dealer who started the club by placing a personals ad in *USA Today* seeking fellow skunk-musk aficionados.)

How can anyone stand skunk musk—much less like it? As an article in *National Wildlife* magazine explains, it is thought that some, shall we say, "nasally challenged" folk can't smell the stinky chemical compounds in skunk musk—but they can smell the undertone odors. One Whiffer, a scientist at the Monell Chemical Senses Center in Philadelphia, reports that skunk musk smells to him exactly like lemonade.

The predilection for skunk musk is indeed rare. Not even skunks like the stench—occasionally, they spray one another while fighting, and the victims beat a malodorous retreat. Even dogs—and here we're talking about creatures that delight in sniffing beneath one another's tails—have been known to retch at the smell. (About the only predator that doesn't seem to mind it is the great horned owl, which preys upon skunks with impunity.)

Precisely because skunk musk is so repellent, it was only a matter of time before someone figured out a way to get people to pay for the stuff. Hunters, trappers and wildlife photographers use diluted skunk musk to mask their own scent. Ray Hanson of Chetek, Wisconsin, ran Skunks Unlimited, catering to that crowd for seven years. (He's since sold the company.) At one point, he tried to market Skunk Guard, a mace substitute that you, like a skunk, could spray at an attacker. To his surprise, Hanson discovered that people were reluctant to spray skunk musk for fear of getting any on themselves.

Rocky Mountain Wildlife Enterprises in LaPorte, Colorado, sells skunk-based Scrooge Christmas Tree Protector to tree farmers to prevent poachers from chopping down their crop. Other clients buy it to spray on abandoned warehouses to discourage drug dealing or in urban cemeteries and parks to deter loitering. A Washington State greenhouse used the product to repel visitors coming over from the drug rehabilitation clinic next door: it turned out that couples were rendezvousing in the nursery's ornamental plants until Scrooge solved the problem.

In fact, says Major Boddicker, who owns Rocky Mountain Wildlife Enterprises, it seems that folks come up with novel uses for skunk scent with each new order. Might we soon be facing a shortage of skunk spray? Fear not, he assures. A skunk holds perhaps three-quarters of an ounce of musk in glands beneath the tail; Boddicker estimates he uses a quart a year, most of it mixed in parts-per-billion with other compounds. A little goes a long way. "That little molecule is so active, you can smell it through plastics, through glass, even through metal," he says. (UPS makes sure his company is the last stop on its pick-up route.) "One-quarter of a quart in the Pentagon would clear the building," he says.

But unless you do something foolish (like kick one of the animals), you can safely and enjoyably watch skunks at fairly close range. Skunks know they are well armed, so they're not trigger-happy. After dusk, they move about with confidence and tolerate human observers exceptionally well. Even the babies display a spunk and persistence that makes watching a family of these creatures one of summer's most delightful spectacles.

During the day, skunks sleep in their dens, often an abandoned groundhog burrow, but at twilight, they venture forth to dig, hunt for mice and play. They will keep at it, snuffling, digging, exploring and mock-fighting, off and on, all night.

New York State Museum's assistant zoologist William Shaw spent the summer of 1927 studying a family of skunks living on a farm near Rensselaer, New York. On a moonlit August night, he described a mother and her four 14-week-old kittens, dashing and lunging, hopping and rolling in play: "Everywhere, there were dashes of white in the half-cloud light of the August moon. It was all so silently and rhythmically done, the only sound produced being that of the back scrape of the paws on the ground."

Skunks aren't always silent, though. The most frequently heard noise from a skunk is a sneeze. This they do to clear their nostrils of earth they have turned up in search of grubs, beetles and ground-living bees. If you find two-inch holes in your lawn, it is a sign that a skunk has been clearing these pests from the turf.

Even if your lawn is intact, chances are a skunk is living nearby. The striped skunk is one of the most widespread and numerous large mammals in North America; one study found that some areas may support as many as 11 of them per acre.

You don't need to live in the country to see skunks. Tracking experts Donald and Lillian Stokes (authors of the Stokes Nature Guides) say they saw more skunks when they lived in the city than when they moved to the country. One regularly ate from their cat's outdoor bowl—often while the cat looked on dolefully.

There's at least one report of a skunk entering a suburban house via the cat door. The state Fisheries and Wildlife Division answered the distress call: the homeowner's young daughter had unintentionally kicked the wandering skunk when she got up at midnight to go to the bathroom. The skunk sprayed in the child's bedroom, and even the wallpaper had to be removed.

Skunks seem so at home around people, you might think a skunk would make a swell pet. Wildlife experts urge you to think again. First, it's illegal to own one in many states—partly because skunks can carry rabies. Also, although skunks can be descented, they never smell like anything most people would want in the house.

And there's one other concern, of which Gloria Bake of West Branch, Michigan, writes in an article titled "Why You Probably Don't Want a Pet Skunk" in *Countryside Journal*: If you have bad breath, your pet skunk might attack your face while you sleep. Mistaking halitosis for the scent of rotting meat, "the skunk is drawn by the odor, and will paw at and attempt to enter your mouth to clean away the leftovers." Painful scratches, she said, can result.

Skunks are best enjoyed outside; besides, little can rival the delights of getting to know a wild animal on its own terms. William Shaw wrote about one particular baby skunk that he watched on an August evening: "Now she would venture quite near, then retreat, to return sniffing and gesticulating, occasionally rising on her hind feet in a graceful squirrellike posture, slowly swinging her head about in a most inquisitive way."

In the course of snuffling about for insects, the youngster came close enough to Shaw to claw at his shoes. Then she looked up and saw what was attached to the shoes. Shaw was astonished at her response. With every hair on her striped body extended, in three "grand, bowing, backward sweeps, each with a scraping sound of stiff-set front toes and raking claws, she scratched the sod with a rasping, raking sound. Then, running a little forward and making two more sweeps, she performed a graceful curve toward her den, quite the most spirited and lovely sight one would wish to see in any wild creature."

# Following Firefly Flashes

*Activities outdoors for kids*

E ACH SUMMER, when the warm nights glow with J-shaped yellow flashes, Ed Duensing and his three sons go out to the backyard to call the fireflies. They "talk" to the insects with ordinary flashlights, mimicking the code of light that female fireflies flash to lure males. "It's easy," explains Duensing, a writer, researcher and naturalist. When a flying firefly flashes, count two seconds (one-Mississippi, two-Mississippi), and then, holding a small flashlight close to the ground, turn it on for one second. Almost immediately, the firefly will turn and approach you. Continue the responsive flashing, and soon the firefly will land on your hand.

In their backyard in Milford, New Jersey, Duensing and his kids have called fireflies in from as far as 40 feet away. Sometimes, several fireflies come at once—as well as all the neighborhood kids. Duensing even lures in some teenage friends of his eldest son, 17-year-old Alex. "You ask them, 'You want to see something neat?' And you get the skeptical look on their faces," Duensing says. "Then the firefly starts to come in, and they're totally attentive and amazed. Then they've *got* to do it themselves. It's irresistible."

Duensing, author of *Talking to Fireflies, Shrinking the Moon: A Parent's Guide to Nature Activities*, proves an important point with his firefly trick: summertime's wild plants and animals can provide kids with more gee-whiz magic than any video game or TV show.

"You give a kid a choice between watching a live wild animal and a TV show, and they'll choose the wild animal," agrees Duke Dawson, program director for the New England Science Center in Worcester, Massachusetts. "Playing with nature creates a real sense of discovery. It can really stretch kids' imaginations."

Nature and kids are a natural combination. "For kids, outdoors is the funnest place to be," says Delia Clark, who used to direct children's programming at the Montshire Museum of Science in Norwich, Vermont. "Sticks and stones and puddles and streams is the stuff childhood is made of."

Or so it used to be—when most kids grew up in the country and later taught their own kids the outdoor games and nature skills their parents had taught them. "One hundred years ago, there wasn't a country boy alive who couldn't hypnotize a bullfrog, or a farm girl who wasn't an expert at weaving a chain of daisies," Duensing observes. But these "old-fashioned" pleasures are just as fun for today's kids.

Sadly, some parents may be afraid of letting their kids play with nature. Duensing recalls a colleague's horror when he told her he was taking his family for a swim in a lake. "But there are living things in there!" she exclaimed. "Yes, and I'm going to be one of them," Duensing replied.

"Kids need to discover that the environment is alive," Duensing says, "and know that it's not just a passive backdrop. They need to find out that if they do something, something in the environment will respond, like a conversation. That's what makes nature so much fun."

For instance, you and your child can play with bats—without ever touching one of the winged creatures. You will find bats on summer evenings even in the most densely populated city park, usually in open areas along a stream or riverbank. Toss a small pebble up gently in front of a flying bat. If your aim is good, the bat will immediately sense it with its sonar—the same way it senses the flying insects it eats—and wheel, midair, to power-drive toward the stone. It is almost like flying the bat like a kite. Bats always figure out it's just a stone and veer away at the last minute; they never swallow or catch the pebble. Kids find this irresistible. Flying bats, by the way, will never make the mistake of flying into you, your kids or people's hair. The only precaution: Watch out for falling pebbles!

Try ant watching. Like playing the bat-flying game, this is something your kid can do on city sidewalks as well as in the country or woods, and you needn't touch the animals to enjoy them (especially since some ants, particularly in the Southwest, can bite and sting). With an inexpensive magnifying glass, it is even more entertaining. (E.O. Wilson, the Harvard entomologist who founded the field of sociobiology, keeps 10,000 Amazonian leaf-cutting ants in his office. He says that under magnification, he can sometimes tell individual ants apart.)

You might suggest that your child watch a single ant for a while. A tiny drop of nail polish on the ant helps identify it among its nestmates, Duke Dawson advises. How long will that ant take to find a cookie crumb you leave for it? Run your finger across the path an ant seems to be following and see what happens.

Daddy longlegs make fine playmates. Don't worry, these aren't spiders—spiders have two body segments, the daddies only one— and they can't bite. Show your kids how to handle one. Never pick it up by a leg, or the appendage might come off. Just coax the creature onto your hand. Then stand up. Tap the back of your hand to catapult the daddy longlegs into the air—and watch it turn into a sky diver, using its body as a parachute to float slowly and gently, almost magically, to the ground. Kids will want to try this for themselves, and the insects won't disappoint them.

Younger children, whose tiny hands may not be steady enough to trust with handling a live animal, can still have fun with them. As an alternative to catching the creatures, Delia Clark suggests that youngsters first watch, then imitate the animals around them. Frogs, chipmunks and squirrels are big hits with preschoolers.

Little kids also love treasure hunts, and nature's treasures pro-

vide endless hunting. Give the kids a mission: Find two things
that smell different. Find something prickly. Find something
tickly. Find something hard. Find something smooth. Small children have incredible powers of observation, Clark points out. If
you give 5-, 6- and 7-year-olds each a leaf and have them examine
it in great detail, they'll be able to pick that leaf out of a pile, even
if they are blindfolded. This makes a good game.

  "If you put kids in an interesting outdoor setting, they'll find
neat things to do," Clark says. Your own yard, even if it's only a
sliver of land, can be a wild kingdom for a child. Make it more interesting. Instead of mowing every inch of the lawn, leave a section
to grow up "wild." Put up bird feeders—or let your child make
one (a slab of wood loaded daily with seed will do fine). Don't
"clean up" that woodpile; let your child explore it—and be prepared to admire the finds. Don't worry, says Clark, that your kids'
outdoor time need be tightly structured. When school is out, let
them enjoy their freedom.

# Tide Pools

## *The sea in miniature*

NEAR THE SEASHORE at every rocky beach, tiny universes of plants and animals, teeming with life and glowing with color, go largely unexplored. In psychedelic settings of Day-Glo orange, hot pink, blood-red and electric yellow, a dozen species of animals may be visible within the space of a single square foot—hunting, feeding, traveling, defending territory. The plants look like animals; the animals look like plants. In these little watery worlds, life has worked out arrangements the likes of which you will see nowhere else on Earth.

These are tide pools, each a constantly changing middle zone between land and sea. Here, in the words of Rachel Carson, "all the beauty of the sea is subtly suggested and portrayed in miniature." Yet most summer beachgoers walk right past them. They don't even know the tide pools are there.

Tide pools deeply reward those who stop and look. Go out to the waterline at low tide—the time is printed in the newspaper—and rock-hop to your destination. (Wear sneakers; they will protect your feet and steady you on slippery surfaces.) As the tide recedes, surf-lashed rock basins become calm pools where you can observe underwater life with unrivaled ease and intimacy.

Wait a few minutes to let your eyes penetrate the glare of the sun on the water. Your vision will adapt to the scale and rhythm of the tide pool as it does to the dark. Soon you will see what at first was invisible: Periwinkles and dog whelk snails glide by. Crabs

A CONSTANTLY CHANGING MIDDLE ZONE BETWEEN
THE LAND AND SEA, A TIDE POOL REWARDS
THOSE WHO STOP AND LOOK.

scuttle sideways, claws waving like boxers' gloves, defending their territory. Springtails, charcoal-colored insects that seem covered in velvet, pop to the surface to walk on the water.

Every tide pool is different. Many seem dominated by plants; some, until you look deeper, appear to hold little more than seaweeds, swaying with the waves. Look for the rockweeds and wracks, whose long, leathery, side-branching blades sport natural buoys, air-filled bladders that keep the sun-hungry leaves afloat. Green, red and brown algae create a miniature forest of ribbons, rubbery sheets, tangling threads, tufts, feathers and tubes.

The most colorful "plants" you will see in a tide pool are actually animals. Look for submerged rocks covered with lichenlike masses of bright orange, yellow and red. These are colonies of animals called tunicates.

Anemones, arrayed in colors from bright pink to orange to green and often found in submerged crevices, look like flowers mounted on fat mushroom stalks. But they, too, are animals; the "petals" are tentacles hunting for fleshy food. The anemone stings with its tentacle-petals and eats snails, small fish and plankton. When it captures prey or when it is disturbed, it pulls its tentacles inward, withdrawing into a soft mound that the casual observer can easily overlook.

In the warm calm of low tide, it can be hard to imagine the hellish extremes in the lives of these small creatures. Within a day's time, they must withstand a 40-degree change of temperature, exposure to the drying sun, then cold, pounding waves.

The periwinkle survives the daily drought by withdrawing completely inside its shell. A horny plate called the operculum forms a trapdoor that seals in moisture and protects the little snail from predator crabs and starfish. (You can delight children by coaxing a periwinkle to open its trapdoor as you hold it in your hand. Tell the kids to emit a long whistle—either a tune or a single note. This will keep them still long enough for the periwinkle to relax, stick out its neck and erect the two tentacles atop its head. Whelks, the other common snails in tide pools, won't do this.)

The lashing surf poses a different problem. As Joanne Barrett likes to tell her classes at Odiorne Point State Park near Portsmouth, New Hampshire, one of the themes of life in a tide pool is "hold on tight." Blue mussels attach themselves to rocks with strong anchoring threads called byssus. Others, like sea urchins and starfish, hold fast with elastic tube-feet that end in suction cups.

You will have better luck finding the more elusive creatures if you pick up some of the rocks in the tide pool. "This is where the really neat stuff is," Ray Hetchka always tells the kids who flock to the education programs he coordinates at Odiorne Point. Starfish, for instance, often lie plastered on rocks' undersides; crabs hide in crevices and under rocks. (But remember, he stresses, put the rocks back, and do so gently, for moving them "is like ripping off the roof of someone's house.")

The rock barnacle is perhaps the most firmly attached. It manufactures a sort of glue with which it cements its own head to its rock. Left high and dry by the retreating tide, a barnacle doesn't look much like a live animal; all you can see is its tightly closed shell. When blanketed by seawater, however, the barnacle swings into action. Even though it is anchored to its spot, the animal is not immobile: It opens its shell plates like elevator doors, sticks out a fleshy stalk tipped with featherlike legs and proceeds to scoop passing plankton into its mouth.

Many tide pool creatures are, like their habitat, mutable, capable of Houdini-like transformation in step with the changing sea. The nudibranch, or sea slug, looks like a gumdrop lump when the sea retreats, but when underwater, it resembles a snail wearing a hairy or bristly overcoat instead of a shell. In the sea, its back blossoms with feathery gills and hairlike projections called cerata. Some of these animals grow three inches long. They may be purple, orange, pale yellow or brown. Some are flecked with brown and white; others are translucent white with red cerata.

Exploring and contemplating tide pools can be deeply relaxing. "If you're left there alone, you forget everything else," says

Barrett. "You're just tide-pooling. Time loses meaning."

But don't forget to look up and seaward every once in a while. The tide, remember, could be rising.

# The Sting

*Mosquitoes: The companionable insect*

WHILE THE REST OF US spent summers trying to fend off mosquitoes with swats and sprays, Todd Livdahl struggled with a different problem: He couldn't get his mosquitoes to bite.

He gallantly proffered his arm. He laid out a smorgasbord of mammals and birds. But the little-known *Orthopodomyia signifera* and *Orthopodomyia alba*, two mosquito species that breed in water-filled tree holes, seemingly turned up their proboscises in disdain. "No one has ever gotten them to bite anything," laments the chairman of Clark University's biology department.

Fortunately for us, not all of the world's 3,400 mosquito species bite people—although some warm evenings, it feels as if they do. Throughout the summer, you are likely to be visited by species whose Latin names leave no doubt as to their popularity: there is the perturbing *Coquillettidia perturbans*, the vexing *Aedes vexans* and, what some consider the worst of all, *Aedes solicitans*—a salt-marsh mosquito named after lawyers. It bites more during the day than most, and it won't fly away from even vigorous shooing.

Though mosquitoes originated in the Tropics and the greatest number of species still live there, the farther north you go, the greater the number of individuals. "Our most vivid memories of bloodthirsty mosquitoes," recalled Adrian Forsyth and Ken Myata in *Tropical Nature*, "come not from the Tropics but from pastoral New England woods and idyllic Rocky Mountain meadows." Northern mosquitoes are not only more numerous but generally more annoying in every way: They buzz louder, they land harder, they itch more. Blame this annoyance on lack of monkeys, suggest the authors. For millennia, tropical mosquitoes have had to adopt sneak attacks and soft landings to avoid the dexterous hands of monkeys, kinkajous and coatimundis. "Northern biters exhibit no subtlety in their approach, because no hand or paw will rise to crush them," they write.

By the time you get to the Arctic, things are even worse. Tundra pools hatch hordes of mosquitoes that literally blacken the sky. Canadian researchers have reported a rate of 9,000 bites per minute—sufficient to exsanguinate a scientist completely in two hours.

Oddly, though, for much of its life, any given individual mosquito would make a perfectly fine companion. As larvae, they live harmlessly in water, and they spend most of their adult lives sipping nectar from flowers, pollinating many species. The males never bite. When it comes time to lay eggs, all females bite something, but not necessarily you. Some species of mosquitoes drink only the blood of lizards. Others specialize in birds. No one has figured out what *Orthopodomyia signifera* or *Orthopodomyia alba* like. Livdahl finally gave up in frustration.

Because of their role as disease vectors, mosquitoes are widely studied. Thousands of entomologists and other scientists around the world are presently trying to raise mosquitoes in their laboratories. Not all readily breed in captivity—rather like pandas in zoos. But happily, some 20 years ago, science worked out a way to remove mosquitoes' sexual inhibitions: anesthetize the female, and cut off the male's head; touch their abdomens together, and presto! everything works by reflex. (Incidentally, decapitation doesn't seem to bother many insects. In fact, removing the head from the bloodsucking *Rhodnius* bug of South America increases its life span more than tenfold.)

Generally, mosquitoes are easy to work with in the lab. Some scientists actually grow fond of them. John D. Edman, an entomologist at the University of Massachusetts at Amherst, is sympathetic to their plight. Most mosquitoes that drink human blood would probably prefer something else, he says. Human blood, he notes, is low in isoleucine, an amino acid that female mosquitoes need to build their egg proteins. But we have slaughtered and crowded out so many other species that for many mosquitoes, we are all that's left on the menu. "What's a poor mosquito to do," Edman asks, "but go for the naked ape with the second-rate blood?"

If we were fewer and less destructive, mosquitoes might not be such a bother to us. But we're not, and they are. Mosquitoes kill more humans than any other animal on Earth: one million people die of mosquito-borne malaria each year. Mosquitoes also transmit more than 100 viral diseases, not to mention a host of parasitic diseases causing blindness, deformity and excruciating pain.

The worst part about mosquitoes is not that they bite but that they drool. Viruses, bacteria and parasites are spread via the mosquito's saliva, which it injects beneath your skin in copious amounts. It contains an anticoagulant, without which every meal would clot in its throat and the insect would need the Heimlich maneuver. Proteins in the saliva elicit the itchy welt you get after a mosquito bite, although some people eventually become immune.

Bruce Landers, superintendent of mosquito control of Suffolk County in Massachusetts, says that the welt might be smaller if you let the mosquito finish its meal; ostensibly, it will suck up most of its own saliva with the last sip of your blood. Plus, if you can stand it, a feeding mosquito is rather interesting to watch.

The mosquito's proboscis looks like a straw, but actually, it is a top and bottom lip, four sets of cutters and a saliva-injecting syringe, all so thin and long that the whole shebang can be inserted into the skin. Then the cutters saw back and forth through the tissue, slicing small blood vessels open. An undisturbed mosquito will thrust and withdraw her mouthparts 5 to 10 times before locating enough blood for a full meal. Often, she will insert the proboscis bent back toward her body, and then she will have to stand on only her rear legs to feed so that the proboscis can straighten out. If you let her feed till full, her abdomen, filled with four times her own weight in blood, will look like a red Christmas tree light, and she'll fly away logy.

What is the best way to get rid of mosquitoes? One solution: more mosquitoes. *Anopheles barberi* is our friend. Unlike most other mosquito larvae, which are filter-feeders, this one is predatory and preys on newly hatched larvae of other mosquitoes. One young *A. barberi* can eat up to 100 other mosquito larvae per day, and better yet, Todd Livdahl notes affectionately, "They go on slaughter rampages." Under certain circumstances, they will, weasellike, kill more than they can eat. Unfortunately, these shy mosquitoes are rare, hatching only in dark, rotten tree holes.

One thing that does not work against mosquitoes, says mosquito-control expert Landers, is lighted electrified traps. "They tend to draw more mosquitoes into the vicinity of the light," he explains. His advice: "Give it to your neighbor."

# History in Stone

*How to read fossils and rocks*

**O**N LAND, it walked upright on two legs. But in the warm, swampy water, it swam with a kind of galloping rhythm, the right foot stepping out longer than the left. The creature occasionally kicked the shallow, muddy bottom with the claws of its three-toed back feet. Then it came to the point where the water deepened, and the 10-foot-long dinosaur lifted clear of the bottom to swim away into watery weightlessness.

This happened 200 million years ago, near Hartford, Connecticut. There were no people, no other mammals; even grass had not yet evolved. But there was mud—mud that is now rock. And from rock, we can read, sometimes with surprising intimacy, the great and small events of the Earth.

Rock turns bone to stone, preserves footprints, petrifies fish; rock captures the air bubbles of liquid lava, records the pressure of colliding continents, tells of the whoosh and swirl of ancient streams.

"There's a story in every rock," says Richard Little, a professor of geology at Greenfield (Massachusetts) Community College. By looking carefully at rocks and rock formations, you can begin to read those stories; and if you split open a rock with a hammer to look inside, you will be the first person in the world to read the story that particular rock has to tell. "Once you know just a little bit of geology," says Little, "the whole world opens up to you."

The best places for collecting rocks are along streambeds and at the beach. These rocks were brought from near and far by water and deposited by the glaciers that covered the continent during the Ice Age, which began two million years ago and ended about 10,000 years ago. A good field guide, such as the Peterson or Golden guide, will help you identify them.

There are hundreds of kinds of rocks, but only three large categories:

**Igneous rocks,** usually massive and hard, are formed when material melts and then cools. Some, like granite, originated in molten pools underground; granite's sparkly minerals formed as the rock slowly cooled and solidified. Another type of igneous rock, basalt lava, often appears as black bands running through other rocks. Many of the tide pools along the North American coasts are old basalt flows.

**Metamorphic rocks,** which often show bands of light and dark minerals, are rocks changed from one form to another by high pressure. Under the heat and pressure of mountain building, sandstone becomes quartzite, limestone becomes marble; often, the pressure creates beautiful swirling bands, such as those seen in gray-and-white gneiss. Sometimes minerals gleam from these metamorphic rocks: schist shines with mica (the same mineral that makes beach sand sparkle) and may also glow with red garnets.

**Sedimentary rocks,** as Little puts it, are "eroded pieces of mountains"—gravel, sand and mud that were washed by dinosaur-era streams into valleys. The layers of sediment compacted, and their grains hardened into rock. Marine muds, rich in seashell calcium, become limestone; petrified sands turn to sandstone; gravel becomes conglomerate.

A rock's type bespeaks how the rock was born. Other features may chronicle its history. In the Northeast, for instance, one story line to look for is written by the glaciers, sheets that covered the land with ice more than two miles deep during the ages when mammoths, shaggy rhinos and giant camels roamed North America.

If you look carefully along the large slabs of granite in northeast mountains, you will often see the scrape marks left by boulder-pocked glaciers. These long impressions look as if the rock were clawed by some monster slipping downslope, desperate for a handhold. The scrape marks are generally parallel, unlike the rougher, more irregular marks left by a bulldozer.

Sometimes, the shape of a rock tells its history. If you find a perfectly round rock, particularly an oddball among many jagged rocks, it may well have come from the bottom of an ancient waterfall or stream channel. Small rocks (basketball-sized or smaller) that become trapped in these spots often act as drills, scouring out stream potholes and waterfall-lunge pools. They are known as "tool rocks," though they were never used as tools by humans.

Sedimentary rocks, on the other hand, often have history thrust upon them. These are the rocks that record where dinosaurs stepped, where bones petrified, where fishes died—these are the fossils.

The Southwest desert is blessed with vast dinosaur boneyards, among the richest in the world. But bones, prints and fossil-fish impressions may turn up virtually anywhere in North America. And the experience of finding a fossil often proves unexpectedly thrilling.

"Who would believe that such a register lay buried in the strata?" fossil hunter and geologist Edward Hitchcock, a professor at Amherst College in Massachusetts, wrote in amazement in 1858. "To open the leaves, then unroll the papyrus, has been an intensely interesting though difficult work, having all the excitement and marvelous developments of a romance."

He was writing about his studies of footprints discovered in shale in Greenfield, Massachusetts. At the time, he was convinced the ancient footprints showed that the area had once been populated by giant, flightless birds and "marsupialoid" animals. Instead, the prints belong to dinosaurs. They can turn up in the most unlikely places too. In 1973, for instance, when Bill Gringas was removing shale to make room for a new deck for his home in Grandy, Massachusetts, he discovered three-foot-long prints of a

50-foot-long dinosaur the size of *Tyrannosaurus.*

Along the beds of certain rivers, "fossil fishing" may prove the most fruitful way to discover these records. Geologist Little advises, "Look for dark shales of the oxygen-poor former lake bottom. With a hammer, split carefully along the layers, and you may be rewarded with coal-black impressions of fish scale, fins or the supreme catch—a whole specimen over two feet long!"

Another plus of geologizing: all that hammering is probably good for you. A few years back, a survey of the obituaries in the journal *Science* revealed that geologists had, with the exception of one killed in a rock avalanche, lived longer than other scientists.

Little offers one theory why: "Geologists are getting the physical release of hammering all these rocks. It feels good."

# Alien Invasion

*Nonnative plants
that dominate the landscape*

S OUNDLESSLY the invaders came, to wage their battles across the American landscape. They arrived from all over the globe: from Russia, Europe, Asia, even Africa. Clothed in luxurious garb of petal and leaf, some foreign plants were carried by the colonists and carefully nurtured; others hitchhiked as seeds hidden in the food of livestock or in the soil used as ballast in old ships and then dumped on our shores.

Today, foreign plants have so insinuated themselves into the American landscape that in some cases, they define it: most people consider bright blue chicory, oxeye daisies, Queen Anne's lace, dandelions and crabgrass as "typical American" plants; Los Angeles is well known for its palm trees. But none of these plant species existed in pre-Colonial America. American fields, forests and marshes are filled with invaders and vagabonds.

While many of these plants have been around for more than two centuries, biologists say their numbers have skyrocketed in the past 20 years. With an explosion in bulldozing, road building and other construction, the opportunistic aliens quickly colonize the altered landscape, taking over drained and flooded wetlands, roadsides and cleared lots. Trucks and railways hasten their spread, carrying seeds of the foreigners in hayloads. As a result, foreign plants that gained a toehold a century or two ago have run rampant; new introductions take off almost immediately.

Some of these aliens, such as oxeye daisies, have become

among our most beloved wildflowers. But other foreign plants have become public enemies—clogging waterways, disrupting natural ecosystems and strangling agricultural crops. According to the USDA, the 10 most serious crop-threatening weeds in America today are all foreign plants; American farmers lose more than $10 billion worth of crops each year to introduced weeds.

The invaders are so successful because in coming here, "they left their own biological control agents behind," says Gerald Henke, a U.S. Forest Service range conservationist responsible for noxious-weed control. Without predators like the insects that kept their numbers in check at home, the aliens spread unimpeded.

"They keep expanding exponentially," says Norm Reese, a USDA research scientist in Montana. Take, for example, leafy spurge, a toxic Eurasian plant that sickens cattle and irritates skin. "In the '40s, a few places started finding it. In the '50s, it was classified as a noxious weed. And in the 1980s, all of a sudden you realized you were in serious trouble." Now the weed is found from California to New York.

In Alabama, kudzu, a high-climbing Japanese vine, covers trees, railroad beds, cars, buildings—"anything that sits still long enough," according to Dr. Jim Miller of the U.S. Forest Service at Auburn. Growing at the horror-movie rate of a foot a day, it fetters stationary railroad cars, overtakes homes and brings down transformers and telephone wires with its weight. The vine's spread, Miller estimates, is costing Alabama, Georgia and Mississippi between $50 million and $175 million a year in lost timber revenues alone.

In Massachusetts, the attractive purple loosestrife, a Mediterranean native with a tall crown of pink-purple flowers, has rendered some waterways in wildlife refuges virtually useless. Taking over marshes and ponds once inhabited by American cattails, bulrushes and sedge, purple loosestrife has usurped the native plants that provided food and cover for rare native birds like the American bittern, the common moorhen and the king and sora rails. Where loosestrife now reigns, these birds have vanished.

In North Carolina, multiflora rose, a bush imported from east-ern Asia, has overrun more than two million acres of meadow. The spine-covered beauty was once encouraged as a natural fence; to-day, it envelopes the fields it was supposed to enclose, rendering them impassable and useless to man and beast.

Perhaps the greatest irony of the alien invasion is that many of the noxious plants arrived as pampered, invited guests, intention-ally imported and carefully nurtured by Colonists and their fol-lowers. Even folk hero Johnny Appleseed was guilty of this mis-take. Besides leaving behind orchards, he also introduced a nasty weed—dog fennel—that plagues Midwestern farmers to this day.

Today, farmers, foresters and agricultural agents are discovering that many of the plants they encouraged are now nearly impossible to get rid of. Kudzu, for instance, was introduced to the South in the 1920s as a forage crop for pigs, goats and cattle—a situation Jim Miller likens to "taking a lion cub home for a pet." By the 1970s, its graceful purple blossoms had overrun seven million acres in Alabama, Georgia and Mississippi, covering fields, forests and homes. "I get calls from little old ladies who tell me their hus-bands have died and the kudzu's taking over their houses. They get nightmares about it," Miller says. By the time kudzu was recognized as a problem, many patches had developed root systems weighing up to 300 pounds, stretching 20 feet underground.

Managers of the Parker River National Wildlife Refuge on Plum Island in Massachusetts are still trying to figure out what to do about the purple loosestrife choking their three freshwater im-poundments. Saving the pools from total takeover, explains Bob Secatore, assistant manager of the 4,650-acre bird sanctuary, "isn't just a matter of dollars, it's how to go about it." Burning or run-ning over it with tractors won't kill it, and little data are available on pesticides' effectiveness on loosestrife.

Getting rid of some of the unwanted aliens has called for some unusual approaches. Hydrilla, an aquatic weed imported from Central Africa and Southeast Asia as an aquarium plant, spread through 200,000 miles of California and Florida canal and river systems until many waterways were completely clogged. To the rescue came a hydrilla-eating fish, the grass carp. (The carp are sterile hybrids, so they cannot become pests themselves.)

USDA researchers have also tried importing foreign bugs to eat foreign plants, but scientists have to be extremely careful they don't select solutions that become worse than the problem. For instance, to try to check the growth of the musk thistle, a thorny weed from Europe with bright pink flowers that grows up to eight feet tall, researchers looked at 89 species of foreign insects known to feed on the plant. Of those, only 26 were detrimental to the weed, but 21 of those species could also damage the U.S. artichoke crop, a plant distantly related to the musk thistle.

Some insect controls have proved very useful; one European beetle, *Chrysolina quadrigemina*, has cut the spread of the Klamath weed (a.k.a. goatweed) by 90 percent. The Eurasian plant's oil glands sicken cattle, and it was such a serious threat to western rangeland that during World War II, banks would not loan on Californian properties infested with it. A statue of the beetle now stands in tribute to its success.

Many scientists agree that most of the foreign plants which have already become well established are here to stay. But at least there is this consolation: we gave Europe poison ivy.

# Nature's Fireworks
*The phenomenal power of lightning*

L UCILLE AND SAL PERESCHINO woke around midnight, when the air conditioner in their Johnston, Rhode Island, home shut off. A summer lightning storm had cut their electricity, the couple realized; but they saw a light coming from the kitchen. They crept down the hall to investigate.

What they saw looked like some sort of science fiction nightmare: Bouncing on the linoleum kitchen floor were tiny orange fireballs smaller than a fingertip. Then they vanished. "We were petrified," Lucille told a reporter after the incident in 1972. They sold the house.

What the Pereschinos saw is known as ball lightning—small, apparently harmless fireballs that typically come popping out of wall sockets, zooming through airline windows, zipping down chimneys. They bounce around, sparkling, and then disappear— often with a loud pop. "Many people don't believe in it," says Massachusetts Institute of Technology meteorologist Earle Williams; but there are so many reliable eyewitness reports of ball lightning, he said, "you almost have to believe it's a real phenomenon."

Certainly, lightning experts have seen lightning do even stranger things: like light up the wings of aircraft, the masts of ships or even the fingertips of scientists with an eerie, sizzling, flame-shaped green glow. This is known as St. Elmo's fire—a phenomenon so weird that Mediterranean sailors long believed the ghostly light was the embodiment of a third-century saint come to protect them from the storm.

Lightning can make a tree branch explode like a firecracker, blow a person's shoes and socks off his feet or make him leap into the air like a marionette. Lightning makes the impossible possible; and summer, with its fast-rising, anvil-shaped, dark thunderclouds, gives birth to most of North America's lightning storms.

When you see these clouds gathering, go inside and watch the show. "Nature's most beautiful fireworks," is how Martin Uman, professor of electrical engineering at the University of Florida in Gainesville, describes these bolts from the blue. Watching a thunderstorm affords a look into the inner workings of a cloud that is generating the force of a nuclear power plant. You'll be witnessing an event that virtually defines the supernatural: lightning is nature at the height of its power, a heavenly display of seemingly infinite energy and light.

A single flash of lightning shines as brightly as a million 100-watt light bulbs, heats the air hotter than the surface of the sun and carries enough electricity to run 20,000 toaster ovens. No wonder cultures around the world have interpreted lightning and thunder as direct evidence of gods at work.

Lightning can be deadly. It kills about 80 people in the United States each year, most of whom are outside. Golfers, the tallest things on a flat fairway, are frequent victims: wearing metal cleats and carrying metal clubs, their bodies become ideal conductors of electricity. If you are indoors, talking on the telephone or using an electrical appliance during a storm can also make you a target.

Yet for all its power, lightning is surprisingly benign. Although at this moment, 1,800 storms around the world are producing 100 lightning flashes per second, three-quarters of all lightning never touches the ground. Instead, it flashes between clouds or within the cloud where it was born. (This often shows up as "heat lightning" or "sheet lightning"—a flash hidden from direct view that is seen reflected from clouds.) Lightning does not kill everyone it strikes; 66 percent, in fact, recover instantly without a wound or scar.

Lightning, like the gods, can be beneficent as well as terrifying.

It prunes forests, taking out the tallest trees so younger ones can grow. Were it not for lightning, says Uman, Florida's forests would have no oaks, for the tall pines would shade them all out. Lightning also fertilizes the soil. Purdue University agronomist David Mengle credits 1992's copious thunderbolts for Indiana's record growing season that summer: each lightning strike transforms hydrogen and nitrogen into ammonia, a natural fertilizer.

Lightning forms in a thundercloud when positive and negative charges become separated—though why the charges separate no one really knows. The positive charges stay near the top of the towering, flat-topped cloud, while the negative charges accumulate near the bottom. When the cloud's bottom charge becomes strong enough, a flow of electricity zigzags down toward the ground. This flow of energy is not the lightning stroke, however. Barely visible and lasting only a microsecond, this is called a stepped leader. Because opposites attract, positive charges from the ground come racing toward the negatively charged stepped leader. The region of positive charge moves up through any conducting objects in the area—including trees, electrical wires and people. It is this brilliant return stroke—coming from the Earth to the sky—that closes the electrical circuit, causing the celestial fireworks of lightning.

The flash appears to be going down because it retraces the downward-forking path of the stepped leader. What seems to be a single flickering flash is actually often a dozen or more strokes, each one only ten-thousandths of a second long, in the same path.

After the flash, you hear the crack and rumble of thunder. The closer the lightning, the more rapid the report of the thunder, the shock wave of air exploding in the 50,000-degree-Fahrenheit heat of the flash. By listening to the thunder, you can estimate how far away the lightning is. (Sound travels much slower than light: in the one second it takes sound to travel four city blocks, light can make it seven times around the world.) Count the seconds between the time you see the flash and the time you hear the thunder. Each second accounts for about 1,000 feet between you and the flash. In five seconds, the sound will have traveled a mile.

Thunder's rumble can also help you measure the length of the lightning channel. The sound will continue all along the lightning's path; if the rumbles continue for 20 seconds, for instance, you will know the lightning bolt was at least four miles long.

The best time to watch a thunderstorm is at dusk, when it is light enough to see the outlines of the clouds yet dark enough to appreciate the lightning. In bright daylight, without special optical detectors, we miss 90 percent of the lightning flashes a storm has to offer, Uman says. Look for the earliest flickers near the top of the thundercloud; then watch the flashes move deeper and deeper into the cloud. If you have a choice of thunderclouds to watch, pick the tallest one, he advises. A cloud twice as deep will produce 30 times more lightning.

The ancients watched lightning carefully, reading in its strikes good luck and bad. One fellow in Maine claims that lightning definitely brought him good luck: On a June day when he was 62 years old, his hearing, his sight—and even his hair—returned after he was struck by lightning.

# AUTUMN

# The Magic
# of Mushrooms

*A kingdom all their own*

**T**HEIR EMERGENCE is almost magical: on an early-fall day, you will find they have mysteriously appeared, full-grown, without warning. Within days, they are gone again. Their variety of form is almost unbelievable. Some resemble parasols, lace, orange peels, petals, tongues, ears, corals or Danish pastries. Some are so strange and wondrous that, in the words of one naturalist, "one is struck incredulous: can such things really be?"

They are mushrooms—fabulous creatures neither plant nor animal, but in a kingdom (Fungi) all their own—and at no time of year are they so abundant, varied and spectacular as in early fall.

At Antioch/New England Graduate School, mycologist Rick Van de Poll's students comb New Hampshire's woods, bogs and lawns for the fleshy fruits of fungi. So eager are they to find, prod, pick, examine and, in many cases, eat wild mushrooms that the one student who *didn't* stands out in Van de Poll's mind. He recalls asking him why he seemed afraid even to touch the mushrooms that the rest of the class so avidly collected. The reply was: "Don't they *hurt* you?"

For the record: No mushroom has ever attacked a person, even when provoked. Touching mushrooms does not produce poisoning, rashes or warts. And of the thousands of North American mushroom species, only six are known to be deadly poisonous to eat. Many dozens are edible, and many thousands are strikingly beautiful. All are ecologically important, giving back nutrients to the earth and enhancing the lives of trees, herbs and flowers.

Yet, alas, many of us are, as David Arora puts it in his book, *Mushrooms Demystified,* "fungophobic." D.H. Lawrence compared the mushroom to what he considered those most loathsome of creatures, the British bourgeoisie. Sir Arthur Conan Doyle, creator of Sherlock Holmes, peppered his written landscapes with mushrooms only when he wanted to create an air of gloom and death. Emily Dickinson insulted mushrooms in a short poem:

> *Had nature any outcast face*
> *Could she a son condemn*
> *Had nature an Iscariot*
> *That mushroom—it is him.*

Continental Europe is far more sensible about matters mushroomic. Russians, for instance, extol the mushroom for "the beauty of its evanescent colors, in the delicate perfection of its gills or pores or skin that are a joy to touch," writes Valentina Pavlovna Wasson. She rhapsodizes over mushrooms for two 200-page volumes in her 1957 work, *Mushrooms, Russia and History.* (Unfortunately, we find no historical evidence here that the democratic revolution can be credited to the simultaneous start of the mushroom season. This is pure coincidence.)

Wasson instructs us that the proper stance for mushrooming is modeled after the Russian peasant woman, who is most often seen foraging in woods or meadows in early fall, especially after a rain, "progressing slowly, stooping and peering to right and left, with a low, circular, sweeping glance, as though she has lost something. She is armed with a hamper and a walking stick to poke here and there; and she springs forward occasionally with a happy pounce and kneels to gather in the prize."

For the Russian peasant, the sought-after prize is the bosky taste of an edible mushroom. But fungi offer foragers many other savory sensory experiences. From a basket holding 45 species that his class gathered in a 15-minute foray through the woods, Van de

STRIKINGLY BEAUTIFUL, MUSHROOMS ARE ALSO
ECOLOGICALLY IMPORTANT, GIVING NUTRIENTS
BACK TO THE EARTH.

Poll picks up a mushroom and draws it under his nose, as if inhaling the aroma of a fine cigar. "Ah!" The blue-green *Clitocybe odora* smells like anise; the yellow russula, a mountain-loving mushroom with a round yellow cap, smells like maraschino cherries; the little brown garlic mushroom, often found on rotting oak leaves, smells, appropriately, like garlic. "Fungi offer a total sensory experience," Van de Poll says: "texture, color, taste, smell."

This makes foraging for mushrooms even more entertaining than an Easter-egg hunt. (Wasson remembers that a traditional punishment for naughty Russian children is to forbid them to go mushroom hunting.)

Kids love to kick puffballs, those big, balloon-shaped mushrooms, to release clouds of powdery spores on impact. (This doesn't hurt the organism at all, because the mushroom is only the fruit of the fungus, not the fungus itself. To pluck a mushroom hurts it no more than picking an apple hurts an apple tree.) Other mushrooms' more gradual release of spores can spawn art. To make attractive "spore prints" from a mushroom, remove the stem, or stipe, and place the cap, underside down, on white paper. In two to six hours, you will have a colored print reflecting the architecture of its underside. Mycologists often use this technique to help identify mushrooms by the color of the spore prints.

With a stick, you can write and draw on some mushrooms and fungi. Many "stain" or "bleed" exotic colors when scratched. The yellow underside of the butter bolete stains blue. The white underside of the fan-shaped, woody artist's conk—a shelflike fungus found in dead or dying trees—bruises brown when scratched. (This big fungus, which can grow to 55 inches across, may warn you when a tree might fall: it grows only on dead or dying trees, and those afflicted with it blow over easily. So if one appears near your house, take heed.)

Mushrooms have served humans throughout history. They've provided food for the peasant, drugs for the psychedelic and—well, we can't deny it—weapons for the murderer. "A pot of mushrooms changed the history of Europe," Voltaire declared. Celebrated victims of poisonous mushrooms have included Roman Emperor Claudius in 54 A.D. and German Emperor Charles VI, whose end precipitated the war of the Austrian succession in 1740.

So, go ahead and indulge your senses. Find, examine, pick, touch and smell all the mushrooms you can—just don't swallow any without the advice of a knowledgeable forager.

# In Praise of Flies

*Rethinking a bothersome insect*

Elizabeth Marshall Thomas, author, anthropologist and animal behaviorist, is best known for her studies of big mammals: elephants, lions, wild dogs and the like. But one brisk October day in her kitchen, her attention turned to a creature many would consider beneath notice. She was watching a fly in the room.

Three flies were in the kitchen that day: two large, one small. What caught her attention was that when Thomas left the room, the small fly followed her. It followed her into the dining room. It followed her into the living room. "For 30 minutes, wherever I was, it was," she observed. "If I was reading, it would be soaring above me or resting on the table. I don't know why it was staying near me. There was no facile explanation."

Thomas, like most of us, simply used to swat the flies that came into her house each autumn. No more. As a result of that October's encounter, "I realized," she said, "flies were more interesting than I supposed."

So fascinating are flies that their activities have occupied some of mankind's greatest minds: Aristotle, for instance, is said to have enjoyed watching flies. Shakespeare has his King Lear speak favorably of them. "Gruesomely delightful" is how former Harvard entomologist Howard Ensign Evans describes flies in his *Life on a Little-Known Planet* (a book he dedicates to the book lice and silverfish in his office). If you watch flies carefully, he promises, you will find "there is much more to the story than merely flying around and looking for a mate or a source of food."

Some flies produce sounds with their wings and use these to communicate with other flies. Some dance. Some hunt. Some make offerings: Males of one European species of dance fly gather insects and pieces of flowers from running water and present them to females like bouquets.

Flies offer almost endless possibilities: There are more than 16,000 species of flies in North America alone (including mosquitoes and gnats, which belong to the fly family). Outdoors, flies are difficult to watch for long because they fly so fast and so far. Horseflies have been observed to circle a car going 40 miles per hour and then land on it. Driven indoors by autumn's chill, however, flies go into slow motion and delight the armchair naturalist. Most species that come inside are preparing to die or hibernate.

Flies are easier to watch in this somewhat groggy state. One of the interesting activities you will see is grooming. Despite their reputation as filthy creatures, flies are fastidious about their own bodies. "Flies are very clean because their lives depend on being clean," says University of Massachusetts zoologist Vincent Dethier. And he should know; he's watched flies for decades and even authored two books on them, *To Know a Fly* and *The Hungry Fly.*

Flies groom frequently and carefully. Dirt on a fly's wings will have the same effect as ice on the wings of an airplane. Dirt on its feet means the fly can't taste—its organs of taste are there. Dirt on any of the fine hairs covering the fly's body clogs its organs of smell. And because flies need keen vision to detect predators like spiders, birds and your flyswatter, they have hundreds of eyes massed in the two bulging sense organs in front of their heads—but no eyelids with which to clean them. What we do with a blink, they must do with their feet.

With a back set of legs, they groom the abdomen. A middle set cleans the wings. The front legs, the equivalent of our hands, work on the eyes, antennae and rest of the face—or so it appears. "The tricky question is," says Dethier, "is it cleaning its head on its feet or its feet on its head?" He suspects that flies, like us, do the former. His observations show that flies typically clean their eyes first and then their front feet—using a motion just like a person soaping his hands. Interestingly, notes Dethier, the fly will also groom the site of an injury, sometimes for hours, much like a person rubs an aching muscle or a sore eye.

Watch a fly looking for food. It is worth providing a small puddle of sugar water to see what happens. The fly scents the meal while airborne. Next it lands to taste the food with a foot. If it approves, the fly will turn in the direction of that foot and lower its mouth to the food.

How the fly eats depends on the consistency of the meal. If the food is liquid, it will suck it up as we would drink from a straw. If the food is solid, the fly has other ways to tackle it. Few people realize that inside its lips, the fly has teeth. Confronted with a lump of dry sugar, "the fly curls its lips as if in a snarl," as Dethier puts it, and then scrapes the sugar with its teeth. Or it can dissolve the sugar—by throwing up on it. (Those white spots you see inside light fixtures are fly vomit.)

There are flies that drink from pools of crude oil. There are flies that live only in coffins. There are, in fact, more than 80,000 different kinds of flies on Earth. Most of them do not come into your house. Here's a guide to a few of the large flies that do:

**Houseflies:** These relatively small, gray flies are the first to come inside for the winter. They often land on your food. Only a few will survive till spring.

**Bluebottle Flies:** This big, handsome fly's scientific name, *Calliphora,* means "beauty bearer." They are hairier and bigger than houseflies and more likely to come into your house in fall than are greenbottle flies.

**Greenbottle Flies:** Big, iridescent, greenish orange flies which buzz so loudly that one fly makes you think the room is full of them. Like bluebottle flies, if they get in the house, they will hang around the dog's or cat's dish. They eat and lay eggs on carrion.

**Cluster Flies:** "Looks like a Lamborghini," according to University of Massachusetts entomologist John Stoffolano. This spiffy gray sportster of a fly is long and lean, with curly yellowing hairs on its abdomen. In autumn, you will find these flies buzzing at your window. They cluster by the hundreds in crevices and show up in spring on the inside of the windowsill. They seldom land on food in your house; instead, they sip nectar from flowers.

**Face Flies:** European immigrants that arrived here in 1952, these flies generally come inside when the autumn housefly population is dying down. They will pass the winter in crevices in your house, reviving on mild days.

Happily, unlike spring's blackflies or summer's deerflies, horseflies and mosquitoes, none of the flies you are likely to find in your house in the fall will bite you. "They are all completely harmless," assures Stoffolano.

If your house is warm enough, you may have a few active houseflies keeping you company all winter. Other flies, however, will spend most of their time in your house trying to escape it. Cluster flies, for instance, will buzz desperately at windows until you either swat them or let them out. Like many kinds of bats and snakes, they spend the winter hibernating among thousands of their kind. They flock to traditional hibernacula, which are used each winter for many generations. Your attic may be one—especially if yours is a white farmhouse on a hill.

If your house doesn't have an attic, you, and the flies, may be out of luck. Entomologist Stoffolano got a call from a builder of cathedral-ceilinged homes who wanted to solve the complaints of his clients: Each autumn, they were plagued by "tons of flies." Without an attic, the insects overwinter in the walls—"or worse," said Stoffolano, "hang around the cathedral ceiling where you can't really catch them, where you can't really swat them, trying to get out but only leaving black specks on your white walls." There was little the entomologist could do.

Not all fly behavior is this easy to decode. Elizabeth Marshall Thomas never did figure out why the small fly followed her around the house; the insects have also confounded British Museum fly expert Harold Oldroyd. In his classic *The Natural*

*History of Flies,* he describes his observation of several bluebottle flies in his house. He noticed them "flying ceaselessly" between two lamps in his living room one evening. He assumed there must be a simple explanation to their movements; surely they were attracted to the light of the lamps. But the next day, he found them flying between the same two lamps in the daytime, when the lights were off. "The only thing one can say about a bluebottle," he concluded, "is that it is prey to conflicting desires."

# Animals on the Move

### *Nature's migrants*

S IT OUTSIDE on clear, star-sparkling nights, and you will hear it: the twittering of thousands of night-migrating birds. Even in urban areas, over the noise of traffic, good ears can pick out the high-pitched, thin *chip* notes of warblers, the *link* call of bobolinks, the soft, lisping *peeps* of the thrushes—south-flying songbirds calling to one another, keeping the flock together through the dark.

Autumn is a time of migration. Animals ranging from dragonflies to whales are on the move. You will see velvety black woolly bear caterpillars (whose brown center band, if wide, is said to foretell a harsh winter) wandering across roads. During an autumn downpour, frogs may literally cover the roads.

And right about this time, fat green darner dragonflies, monarch butterflies and broad-winged hawks are all traveling roughly the same route south for the winter. The insects are heading for Mexico; the broad-wings will continue on to South America.

For a woolly bear caterpillar, "its migration of 500 yards is as dangerous as a hawk's flying to South America," says Tom Tyning, master naturalist with the Massachusetts Audubon Society. Woolly bear caterpillars, which are the larvae of tiger moths, don't spin cocoons or pupate for the winter; they must wander in search of a good spot to burrow into the leaf litter. They will emerge, still caterpillars, in the spring.

Some frogs, like wood frogs and peepers, also spend the winter in leaf litter; they survive the frigid months frozen solid. Other frogs, including the leopard frog and the bullfrog, travel to new ponds. When the surface has frozen, you may see these frogs through the ice, swimming near the bottom.

One of the greatest spectacles in autumn is the sight of hundreds of thousands of birds of prey funneling down from the north along North America's great aerial pathways, or flyways, heading for Central and South America. Soaring on thermals—rising columns of hot air—inland hawks ride the air currents, sometimes to 15,000 feet or higher, as if on a spiral escalator, and then set off south in a shallow glide. With a good tail wind, falcons may reach speeds of more than 100 miles per hour without flapping.

Normally, these predatory birds are solitary hunters; but this time of year, because they are all looking for thermals to ride, you may see hundreds or even thousands massed together, "kettling up" on a rising thermal like wind made visible. From a field with a wide view, as the air is warmed by the sun between 9 and 10 a.m., you may see hundreds of broad-wings lifting off from surrounding woods.

Audubon Societies and local nature centers organize hawk watches in many areas around the country. Thousands of observers climb up mountains or position themselves along shores from favorite vantage points like Hawk Mountain, Pennsylvania; Point Pelee, Ontario; the Goshute Mountains in Utah; and Cape May, New Jersey. These formal counts are part of a national network tallying up the raptors. In the 1950s, hawk watches provided an early warning of population crashes due to spraying of the pesticide DDT. Today, hawk watches are documenting these species' recovery programs: on a single day in 1991, at Cape May, hawk watches counted 152 peregrine falcons, the most since 1950.

The best times to spot inland hawks like broad-wings, red-tails and turkey vultures is on windy days between 10 a.m. and 3 p.m., when thermals are strongest. The birds' soaring forms show up best against white clouds. With 7-to-10-power binoculars, you may be able to tell whether a bird has breakfasted that morning: Often, you can see the hawk's distended crop, a sort of first stomach at the bottom of the neck, bulging with food.

Simon Perkins, a field ornithologist with the Audubon Society, has watched this spectacle for more than 25 years. For many people, hawks symbolize strength and beauty in nature. But it is their migration, retracing the precise paths their ancestors took millions of years before them, that most deeply moves Perkins. "To this day," he says, "I am still completely awed by this phenomenon."

# Competing for Color

*Fall flowers' subtle beauty*

E VEN BEFORE the leaves have turned, its feather-soft plumes offer the most brilliant golds of autumn. English gardeners prize the goldenrod, cultivating it in perennial borders and showcasing it in indoor flower arrangements. Yet in North America, where fall roadsides, meadows, wetlands and woodlands blaze with more than 100 varieties of this native wildflower, many people moan when they see the plant. Some dig it out of their gardens; few would ever dare bring it inside.

Goldenrod is a stranger in its own land. Often mistaken for a plant it doesn't even resemble, goldenrod is blamed for an ailment it doesn't cause. The inconspicuous green flowers of ragweed bloom at the same time as goldenrod's lavish sprays, but ragweed's pollen is the main cause of hay fever—goldenrod's pollen poses no peril.

"Goldenrod is a very underappreciated plant," says Heather McCargo, who propagates plants for the New England Wild Flower Society. And that's the case with many of our native autumn wildflowers: too often, even though they may be stunningly beautiful, they're underestimated, misunderstood or simply overlooked.

"Most people associate wildflowers with spring, not fall," says Barbara Pryor, who handles public relations for the Wild Flower Society. But for many plants, she explains, flowering in autumn has advantages over flowering in spring: April and May bloomers must set seed before a leafy canopy shades out the sun; fall flowers can bask in the light.

True, more species bloom in spring; but in fall, there are plenty of flowers, and you won't have to suffer through mud and black-flies to find them. "People don't realize," Pryor says, "how much there is to see."

Following cool, wet summers, fall wildflowers are particularly spectacular. Cool summers extend the blooming season for many plants well into autumn, and you may see red and yellow Indian paintbrush, white Queen Anne's lace and black-eyed Susans flowering alongside later-summer and early-fall wildflowers like delicate pink mallow, pink and purple asters and crimson cardinal flower—often all in the same place.

Where should you go to see these beauties? In fall, you will find wildflowers blooming in every habitat, from forests and bogs to meadows. But perhaps best of all, you can also spot up to a dozen species of wildflowers in bloom along a single roadside, in one vacant lot or even on an unmowed portion of your lawn. The charm of wildflowers is their wildness: whether they are true native American plants like goldenrod or, like Queen Anne's lace, the descendants of foreigners that "escaped" cultivation, wildflowers grow where they please, often choosing to flourish in areas people have forsaken.

Wildflowers are more than just beautiful; their bounties range from medicine to entertainment. Take jewelweed, for example. "If nature ran a novelty shop," says New Jersey naturalist and author Ed Duensing, "it would always keep a large supply of jewelweed in stock." And it does. Along the banks of streams, along the edge of any moist, wooded area, you will find loads of these light green two-to-three-foot-tall plants, their conical, speckled-orange flowers hanging down in pairs by threadlike stalks. In his guide to nature activities, *Talking to Fireflies, Shrinking the Moon*, Duensing tells how to thrill children with jewelweed's natural antics.

The flowers set seed and become half-inch blimp-shaped pods. Squeeze one at the base, and you'll send its seeds shooting up to six feet away with an audible pop. When you have popped a few, thrash a stick in the center of the jeweled grove. You'll explode hundreds of pods at once—a spectacle that will look and sound, Duensing promises, "like a giant out-of-control popcorn machine. Children watching this wild event will become absolutely giggly."

More jewel than weed, the plant also provides one of nature's most welcome medicines. The juice in its fat green stems dissolves the oil that causes the itchy, oozing rash of poison ivy. Applied to skin that has touched poison ivy, jewelweed can prevent the rash— or at least soothe it, if it is too late.

Fall wildflowers also provide a window into the lives of other creatures and offer a last chance to see them before they migrate, hibernate or die. Atop purple stems that may tower 10 feet, look for the clusters of cylindrical, pink-purple blooms of stout joe-pye weed (named after a Native American medicine man who used the plant to cure typhus) growing in damp thickets and in meadows along streams. The chances are excellent that you will find a butterfly nectaring among its blooms. Perhaps you will even see a great spangled fritillary—this time of year, they're all widows, laying eggs fertilized by long-dead males.

The milk-bottle-shaped flower of the bottle gentian provides a great chance to watch bees. Cradled in a whorl of four to six narrow pointed leaves, the big blue blossoms on this upright foot-tall plant seem forever budding and never fully open. To get to the nectar, a bee pries open the petals and peers inside. If the nectar has not been taken, the bee climbs inside, the petals slamming shut behind it like a door. You'll see the flower shaking as the bee rattles around inside it. Look for the bottle gentian in moist, shady places. But don't dig it up; unfortunately, it's becoming rare in some parts of the country.

One flower you certainly *can* pick is goldenrod. Few blooms are more lovely in floral arrangements, especially when its graceful shapes combine with the rod-stiff black-eyed Susans and the delicate white rays of small asters. You may still find it blooming into November, when it combines handsomely with dried plants like cattails and the brown, fertile spikes of sensitive fern.

If visitors sneeze at your centerpiece, set them straight. Native Americans considered goldenrod a healing plant. Its Latin name, *Solidago,* means "to make whole." A tea made from the leaves, along with Irish moss, lemon and honey, is said to ease sneezing, runny nose and itchy eyes—the very symptoms for which its flowers are wrongly blamed.

# Leave It to Beavers

*Nature's foremost conservationists*

Y OU WILL HEAR IT before you see anything—a sharp, loud *p-l-oonk*—the tail slap of a beaver. Aware of your presence, the animal slaps the water with its broad, flat tail before diving out of sight, signaling a warning to the rest of the family. If you wait silently, however, the beavers will soon reemerge from the lodge, their square heads streaming above the water.

In autumn, beavers are exceptionally busy. Before the ice freezes over, confining them to their lodges and what water remains navigable below the ice cover, they are gathering a food cache of tasty young branches for winter. They anchor the branches in underwater mud, where the bark and leaves will be preserved for later consumption, as in a watery refrigerator.

Beavers, North America's largest rodents (they grow to more than two feet long), are delightful to watch for their industry and their family affection. For their ecosystem-altering constructions, creating new habitats with their dams, Roger Tory Peterson calls them "nature's foremost conservationists." Yet few animals have been so relentlessly exploited.

In many areas of North America, beaver pelts were the gold standard of the 1700s and 1800s. By 1896, at least 14 American states—Massachusetts, Vermont, New Hampshire, New York, Rhode Island, Connecticut, Pennsylvania, New Jersey, Delaware, Maryland, Illinois, Indiana, West Virginia and Ohio—had announced that all of their beavers had been killed. Thanks to a beaver-recovery program, including live-trapping and relocating to protected areas, beavers have made an impressive comeback throughout the country. "For all practical purposes, they're everywhere," says Tom French of the Massachusetts Division of Fisheries and Wildlife.

But beavers have apparently undergone a major behavioral change since the days of mass-trapping. Early North American explorers' journals reported that beavers were active by daylight, often sunning themselves as they rested atop dams and lodges. Today, beavers are primarily nocturnal, most active from twilight to daybreak.

Naturalist Hope Ryden, whose 1989 book, *Lily Pond,* documents her four-year study of a family of beavers in Upstate New York, concludes this change is a direct response to hunters. Only the stealthiest, wariest beavers have survived—those beavers that confine their activities to darkness. As further evidence for this theory, Ryden cites beavers' extremely poor night vision. Their eyes do not shine red when caught in a beam of light—a glow easily seen in most nocturnal animals, caused by the presence of light-gathering crystals in the retina, the tapetum lucidum.

This means that if you want to watch beavers, you need to visit them in late afternoon or evenings. It is a good idea to stake out an active beaver pond in advance. Look for a dam or a lodge: a mound of large branches and logs, covered with finer branches and vegetation and plastered with mud. The top of the lodge, in which the beaver family sleeps, is not plastered, to allow for ventilation. Lodges may be up to 8 feet high and 40 feet across.

A lodge, however, may be abandoned after the beaver family runs out of food and construction materials in the area. Aspen, alder, birch, sweet gum, poplar and willow are favorites. Only when these are depleted will the beavers resort to eating the bark and leaves of oak and swamp maple and to cutting conifers—which must taste like turpentine—to build their dams. To see whether beavers are in residence, look for trees freshly gnawed in the classic pencil-point shape. (Sometimes, people find gnawings

BEAVERS CUT TREES TO EAT THE BARK AND LEAVES
AND TO GNAW WOOD INTO LENGTHS TO CONSTRUCT
AND REPAIR DAMS AND LODGES.

at a height of five feet or more and conclude that they have discovered the work of a monster beaver. Actually, the tree has been felled in winter by a beaver standing on a snow mound.) Beavers cut trees to eat the bark and leaves of the upper branches and to gnaw wood into small lengths to construct and repair dams and lodges.

Scent mounds and trails are other signs of beavers. In their dexterous, black velvety paws, beavers will carry mud to a spot near the water's edge and then mark it with castoreum, washed from glands beneath the tail with their urine. There may be 40 to 120 of these scent mounds—each up to two feet tall—within a beaver family's range. They are thought to mark a family's defended territory. A beaver's trail, 15 to 20 inches wide, may extend 100 feet away from the water's edge to the feeding area.

Once you have located an active pond, sit quietly by it some evening, preferably when moonlight will outline the beavers in silver. Dress far more warmly than you would for a daytime hike, as you may sit for a long time in the dark, on cold ground, without moving. Take along light-gathering binoculars, if you have them. If not, use a flashlight or even a spotlight; oddly enough, Hope Ryden reported the beaver family she observed did not seem bothered by her high-powered halogen beam.

On late afternoons and early evenings in the fall, beavers tend to concentrate on food gathering. Later in the evening, you may see them playing or repairing their lodges or dams. Frequently, they rearrange branches, cementing them in place with mud or even rocks. Swiss researchers A. Aeschbacker and George Pilleri once left 40 marked branches at a beaver pond to see what the animals would do with them. When they returned a month later, they found the beavers had sorted the lumber by size, to use for specific building requirements. Long sticks, for instance, were used for high-vaulted entryways, smaller ones for lower openings.

Sometimes, you may see an upright bush floating above water, seemingly traveling on its own, powered by an underwater beaver. Or you may watch a beaver heaving a cut tree to the pond, grunting with exertion much like a person would. Occasionally, you may see one beaver swimming with such a woody prize, followed by another member of the family, entreating, *Uh-Uh-Uh-UH-UH-UHH!* Ryden translates this sound, roughly, to the claim, *My stick! MY stick! MY STICK!*

Few other animals offer such paradigms of close-knit family life. Beavers mate for life, and both parents care for the two to three kits born each spring. Littermates remain with the parents for two years, often helping to care for their younger brothers and sisters. Beavers sometimes rub their faces together, Eskimo-style, and "talk," wrote Swedish biologist Lars Wilsson, "the tones and nuances of which seem, to a human, expressive of nothing but intimacy and affection."

Beavers can recognize individual humans at close range and may even leave the water to greet a favored visitor. Toronto-based naturalist R.D. Lawrence rescued an orphaned baby beaver, raised it and released it to the wild; the beaver, whom he called Paddy, would thereafter emerge from the pond at Lawrence's call and greet the naturalist with cheery mumbles.

The late Dorothy Richards of New York's Adirondack Mountains gave four adult beavers the run of her house and converted a downstairs living room into a swimming tank. The animals—including one huge 24-year-old weighing 60 pounds—would frequently sit on her lap.

Tom French knows people who leave out grain and tasty twigs (apples, sweet potatoes and lettuce are also cheerfully accepted) to lure beavers nearer to their homes. "Some people have these 40-pound rodents coming up on their sun porches," he said.

This works fine unless the gnawing rodents eventually decide that the wooden porch might better adorn their lodge or dam.

# Chipmunks and Squirrels

*A ubiquitous source of wildness and wonder*

ABOUT THE TIME people are stacking wood on their porches for winter and bringing in the pumpkin, squash and carrot harvest, animals are doing just about the same thing. Preparing for winter, blue jays, woodpeckers and nuthatches jam seeds into the crevices of trees for storage. Chipmunks stuff their cheek pouches with seeds and nuts at a rate one naturalist calculated to be more than 900 acorns per chipmunk per day.

Gray squirrels are gathering acorns, hickory nuts and, in city parks, foods as diverse as discarded bagels and candy. (Squirrels have a sweet tooth; in woods, they will lap up sweet maple sap from trees, and in city parks, they have been known to raid outdoor candy-vending machines. Observers report they prefer candy bars with nuts.) Red squirrels' eclectic harvests also include mushrooms: on a woodland walk, if you see plucked mushrooms hanging, caps down, from the twigs or crotch of a tree, you can be pretty certain a red squirrel put them there to dry before storage underground.

Autumn's harvest of acorns, pinecones, seeds and nuts affords a wonderful chance to watch these hoarders in action, even if you venture no further than your window. This time of year, chipmunks and squirrels are especially active, a near-at-hand source of wildness and wonder.

Both chipmunks and gray squirrels can be tamed to eat out of your hand; squirrels around Harvard Yard, in fact, almost demand that you feed them. While the shyer red squirrels stick to cone-bearing forests, gray squirrels are found anywhere there are seed- or nut-producing trees. Some are so well adapted to cities that in New York's Central Park, researcher Richard Van Gelder found the squirrels learned to cross the streets just after dawn to avoid their major "predator," the automobile. (In nearby Stuyvesant Square Park, on Manhattan's Lower East Side, squirrels would sometimes wait with pedestrians on sidewalks for the traffic lights to change.)

Chipmunks, on the other hand, are most often found in brushy areas, along stone walls and woodpiles, from woods to sub-urbs. You can call chipmunks by imitating their voices. Simply an-swer a chipmunk's high-pitched *chip!-chip!-chip!* with a comparable kissing sound, and it will usually approach you, standing erect and alert for a closer look, chipping all the while. A chipmunk may keep up this conversation with you for five minutes or more. Often, other chipmunks will chime in.

Chipmunks and squirrels gather and store their food in differ-ent ways. Watch carefully as a gray squirrel selects a nut. It usually picks up the nut in its teeth, then holds it with both paws, puts it back in the mouth, turns it around and moistens it with its tongue. Then the squirrel bounds off to dig a hole with the forepaws, about three inches deep. Holding the nut in its teeth, the animal rams it, point first, into the hole and, with paws and snout, replaces the dirt, then the leaves and finally the grass, combing the blades with both paws so that the hiding place is in-visible. It is thought squirrels relocate these caches by smell.

Chipmunks, by comparison, hardly ever bury nuts. Each stores nonperishable food in the pantry area of its individual burrow. (The only chipmunks that bury food are recently dispersed juve-niles which have not yet excavated a burrow.) You will often see chipmunks racing after each other, defending their foraging terri-tory, which usually extends 75 feet around each burrow. You can tell when the two cross from one's territory to the other's, for at that point, the pursuer suddenly becomes the pursued. If you see a chipmunk with half a tail, you can be reasonably sure it was lost to another chipmunk during a turf squabble.

Donald and Lillian Stokes' Nature Guides rightfully call chipmunks' cheek pouches "marvelous little shopping bags for food." The pouches are located along the cheek and neck just under the skin, and there is an opening to each pouch below the lips and teeth. Because of these expandable cheek pouches, a chipmunk can carry up to 12 large acorns or more than 70 sunflower seeds at a time. Stuffing all that in sometimes takes a bit of finessing. If you watch closely, you can see a chipmunk trim sharp edges from large morsels before placing them in its mouth. A chipmunk will often spit things out, reposition them with its paws and even push on its cheeks from the outside to rearrange things.

Naturalist Lawrence Wishner was so enchanted by the eastern chipmunks in his 1½-acre Virginia backyard that he spent six hours a day for six years watching them. From his efforts, we now know the difference between the meaning of a chipmunk *chip*—an expression of surprise, usually at a ground predator—and the lower-pitched *chuck*—used in anger or annoyance and to announce a hawk alarm.

Wishner also deciphered the meanings of various tail postures and movements. A chipmunk with its tail in the air is alarmed. When involved in investigation, a chipmunk will move its tail horizontally, in whiplike slow motion, sometimes stamping its back feet. And while squirrels flick their tails up and down in annoyance, when a chipmunk does this, you can bet it is a male propositioning a female.

The squirrel's tail is equally revealing, and to keep it fit for its myriad uses, the animal often grooms and fluffs it with paws, teeth and tongue. The appendage serves at various times as a counterbalance during quick turns, an aide to communication, a foil brandished against rivals like a bullfighter's cape and a blanket in cold weather.

Unlike chipmunks, gray squirrels do not hibernate in winter.

Squirrels retreat each night to sleep in tree hollows, sometimes with up to 12 others. If a hollow is not available, they sleep in nests constructed of leaves and woven branches, situated high up in deciduous trees. Called dreys, these nests are easy to spot in winter when tree branches are bare.

After observing chipmunks and squirrels for a while, you will begin to recognize individuals. Look for identifying scars like a notched ear or short tail; field glasses will help you spot more differences in markings. You will then be able to keep up with the lives of these characters for some time—chipmunks typically live two to three years; gray squirrels, six to eight.

# Return of the Wild Turkey

## The successful restoration of these once rare birds

D RIVERS HEADED WEST on the Massachusetts Turnpike, only five miles from the city of Framingham, were alarmed one fall day when they saw eight black objects, nearly the size of armchairs, flying across the road just above the traffic. As it turned out, the objects were wild turkeys.

Standing three to four feet high, weighing as much as 25 pounds and congregating in groups of up to 100, wild turkeys are a stunning sight—particularly as they zoom over highways, flying as fast as a car, or when they appear on city streets, alighting on parked cars. (Some folks let the meter run out rather than risk disturbing the big birds.)

These days, once rare wild turkeys are showing up all over: raiding bird feeders, occasionally roosting on houses (those may not be Santa's reindeer you hear up there) and even breaking off TV antennas with their weight. Late autumn is the best time of year to see these astonishing birds, when trees are bare and the turkeys are most likely to venture into the open for food. Mornings and late afternoons, watch for them as they emerge from the woods. Later in the season, look for their four-inch-long tracks in the snow. Follow the tracks up over a ridge, and you are likely to see turkeys at close range.

Wild turkeys often feed on corn stubble or on grains in manure spread on fields, says Audubon field ornithologist Wayne Petersen; they file out of the woods in a straight line, with the largest turkey leading. "It's an incredible sight," he says. "There's nothing like it."

Once hunted to near extinction, the wild turkey has, with human help, staged one of the most heartening wildlife comebacks in North America. Our great nation now boasts more wild turkeys than there were in 1600, according to the National Wild Turkey Federation, a conservation organization based in South Carolina. Turkeys occupy 49 states—everywhere but Alaska—including 11 states they did not inhabit in Colonial times. They are even found at Cape Canaveral's Kennedy Space Center, reports Gene Smith, the federation's publications director. "Wild turkeys," he is quick to point out, "witness every shuttle launch."

By the 1850s, most of the nation was bereft of wild turkeys, victims of the Colonists' overhunting, lumbering and land-clearing fires. There still existed the oven bird—a different subspecies of the eastern wild turkey, with a tail tipped in white instead of brown—whose now extinct progenitor was originally domesticated by the Aztecs. (Cortez brought that turkey back to Europe, and it returned, fat, flightless and foolish, to North America with the Pilgrims.) But Americans missed the wily magnificence of the wild turkey, and attempts began as early as 1914 to restore it by releasing human-raised offspring of wild birds captured from relic populations in New York and Pennsylvania.

The early efforts failed miserably. In the wild, the young turkeys, though genetically "wild," displayed all the wit and initiative of the self-basting variety. They quickly perished.

The turkey transfers finally took when biologists started trapping adult wild turkeys and releasing them—to raise their own offspring—in turkeyless states. Now there are turkeys all over the place—a comeback which rivals that of the white-tailed deer. The success proved an important point: "Only the mother wild turkey can raise a wild turkey," says Gene Smith.

Mother wild turkeys teach their offspring skills that barnyard fowl never master. With a wingspan that dwarfs an eagle's, a wild turkey can fly 55 miles an hour and glide for three-quarters of a mile. Its wing beats at takeoff can blow your hair back even if you are 15 yards away. The Thanksgiving turkey, on the other hand, might not fly even if you pitched one off a roof.

Wild turkeys, unlike their fatter domestic cousins, are noble birds, reportedly capable of great bravery. In his book *Birds on the Move: A Guide to New England's Avian Invaders,* New Hampshire naturalist Neal Clark relates the startling experience of hunter Ernie Belleville. In 1984, he shot a young turkey in Lee, New Hampshire. As he came in to retrieve the kill, "an older, larger turkey flew at him, hit him at the waist and knocked him backwards. The gobbler then tried to spur him, so he retreated, later finding his stomach black and blue and his leg scarred."

An even more moving instance of courage was uncovered by David Stemple, a professor of computer science at the University of Massachusetts at Amherst, while researching his children's book *High Ridge Gobbler.* Two turkey hens were raising their broods together. One day, a hawk swooped down from the sky, aiming to grab one of the chicks, or poults. The first hen leapt up and met the hawk in the air, knocking it down; then the second hen attacked. The hawk had to struggle to get away.

It is actually fairly common, authorities say, for two turkey mothers to raise their broods together—which seems a good idea, since each hen may hatch 14 to 16 chicks a year. The groupings of birds you are most likely to see this time of year are mothers with their female young, or jennies. Hens kick out their male offspring, or jacks, around October.

According to the turkey federation, in winter, turkeys normally travel in sex-segregated flocks, with young males forming bachelor flocks headed by a more experienced, dominant tom turkey. ("Megaflocks" of 40, 60 or up to 100 birds of both sexes may appear at a favored food source, but when they have finished feeding, they will split up into their smaller family groups.)

If you have found a good turkey-watching spot (often staying in your car is the best bet) and have remembered your binoculars, you can figure out who's who in the flock. The grown toms are fatter and taller than the hens, with redder heads, and sport a long dangling tassel called a beard hanging from the chest. (Hens, like the circus ladies, can also grow beards, but this is rare.) The longer the beard, the older the bird. A very lucky wild tom turkey can live 12 years.

If you have never seen a wild turkey, your first encounter with one will likely be an event you'll remember forever. Computer-science professor Stemple will never forget his first time: He was sitting motionless on the forest floor while a friend, a master turkey caller, voiced the wavering love song of the hen. A big, black bird approached. At nearly four feet tall, the tom turkey towered over the sitting men.

"The only thing I could think of," said Stemple, "was, if the dinosaurs weren't extinct, here was one of them. When they're close up, they're scary."

# WINTER

# Tales of
# the Tree Trunks

*A natural history of the landscape*

WHEN TOM WESSELS was growing up, he used to try to stalk silently through the oak woods behind his Connecticut house, emulating the footsteps of the Indians. But even with soft moccasins, he could never move noiselessly in the fall. "There was no way I could do it without making leaves rustle," he recalls. "I always wondered, how did the Indians do it?"

Not until he was in graduate school studying plant ecology did he find out: the Algonquin, the natives of his beloved New England, could move silently even in autumn because before European settlers arrived, there *were* no dead leaves to crunch and rustle beneath their feet. The Algonquin burned the leaves in fires they set each year—fires that sculpted parklike woodlands utterly different from the thick forests found on their former homelands today.

With that realization, Wessels, now chair of the science department at the Putney School in Vermont, began to see the landscape in terms of a series of stories: of Indians and settlers, of hurricanes and lightning strikes. "There are some amazing stories, and it's really fun to find them out," he says. Once you learn how to read the landscape, the shape of tree trunks, the lie of logs, the species and size of bushes all tell stories of fire, storm and ax.

With summer's wash of green laid bare and before obscuring

snows, early winter is an ideal time to spot the boldest evidence of
the stories your local woods has to tell. You can read history writ
large and small. A juniper tree bears witness to a former sheep pasture. A dent and mound in the earth tells of a storm that might be
hundreds of years past. "There's a whole dynamic going on here,"
Wessels said on a walk through the woods, "and the natural history, which otherwise is piecemeal, makes sense in this frame-
work."

Look at the shape of tree limbs. Most forest trees branch narrow and tall, jealous of light. The exception will stand out: large,
muscular-looking trees, with limbs spread like outstretched arms.
If you come upon such a tree, you have made a discovery. Its shape
testifies to a time when it had the sun to itself. Years ago, it stood
alone in a meadow, providing shade for pastured animals.

Occasionally, you might come upon a hawthorn with an hour-
glass figure. Why the odd shape? Herbivores create this bit of topi-
ary. They eat the tender tips of the hawthorn, first pruning the
young shrub to an almost artificial-looking cone shape; but as the
plant grows above the grazers' reach, the branches can spread out
horizontally again. In the Midwest, hourglass-shaped hawthorns
are a sign of cattle pasture even if the cattle are not immediately in
residence.

Most woods in today's New England were once pasture.
Between 1810 and 1840, three-quarters of central New England
was cleared for pasturing sheep. Napoleon's defeat of Portugal
ended that country's export embargo of Merino sheep, a woolly
race so hardy it could withstand New England winters.

Napoleon is responsible for many of the stone walls you find
in the woods—a legacy of pasture. Another clue is juniper. You
may find this slow-growing low evergreen, often gnarled and
twisted, dying in the shade of young hardwoods. Juniper can grow
only in the crevices of rocks or in pastures; the juniper's presence
recalls vanished sheep, cows or goats, which cropped the herbaceous
plants that would normally outcompete the seeding juniper. In
more southern parts of the country, eastern red cedar signals for-

mer pastures instead of juniper. Why? It can germinate only in turf.

Buffalo and Native Americans shaped the open parklike forests of northern Illinois. Mae Watts, an Illinois naturalist and author, could read their influence in the hawthorns and blackberries growing beneath bur oaks: these are signs of a grazed forest. The bur oak's corky bark withstood the intentional fires; thorned blackberries and hawthorns withstood even buffalo-sized appetites—reasons these species still dominate the area today.

Similarly, in a line of cottonwoods, Watts could see a vanished wagon track in an Indiana sand dune. A row of these trees indicates that cottonwood seeds found shelter and moisture in the tracks of wagon wheels—or, in the case of younger cottonwoods, jeep tires.

Walking through the woods is like solving a mystery. You come across a downed tree. What killed it? Look first at the base of the tree, Wessels advises. A depression, then a mound before the straight trunk stretches out show the roots were ripped from the ground whole—indicating the tree was alive when it fell. This so-called pillow-and-cradle topography can persist thousands of years, long after the tree has rotted.

Are there other downed trees nearby? This can be another clue. If they are all facing in one direction, they were killed in a blow-down—likely a hurricane. Some forests, such as the Pisgah Wilderness in New Hampshire, still preserve big trees downed in the 1938 hurricane. In some areas, notes outdoors educator Neil Jorgensen, from the position of downed trees, you can virtually map the path of hurricanes. Along the East Coast, for instance, you can see the path taken by the counterclockwise-spinning storm as it tore over southern Connecticut, whipped up the Connecticut Valley, then veered northwest over Vermont. East of the hurricane's path, all downed trees point in a northwesterly direction; west of the hurricane's path, they all face southwest. Overturned sawed stumps show how homeowners tried to salvage the downed timber.

A tree killed by fire offers different clues. Fire-killed trees do not show pillow-and-cradle formations, because they may not fall for up to 50 years after they are burned. Fire-killed trees rot very slowly—even the bark of the dead tree will stay on for up to five years. Fire and lightning alter wood to make it resist decay, a fact that early settlers put to use by burning the bases of fenceposts before sticking them into the ground. If you find a number of standing dead trees, they were likely killed by fire, not lightning, and you will be able to see fire scars on living trees in the area. Look on the uphill side of the base of trees for flame-shaped scars, carved by burning leaf litter as it rolled downslope. Some trees are too sensitive to survive a fire. Some authorities believe the Algonquin virtually extinguished beech, hemlock and black birch from many areas with their fires. A mature black birch is a sign that the area hasn't seen a fire in a very long time.

As the Algonquin knew well, however, fire favors certain trees and shrubs: blueberries thrive on burned land; nut-bearing trees, like chestnut, shagbark hickory and red oak, sprout vigorously from charred stumps and often grow multiple trunks as a result.

Hemlock, on the other hand, cannot sprout from its stump, yet sometimes you will find this normally straight-boled evergreen sporting multiple trunks. This clue provides no insight into the larger history of the forest, but it does offer an intimate detail in the biography of that individual tree. It is likely, says Tom Wessels, that the hemlock assumed this shape because of an early injury— probably its bark was nibbled by a porcupine.

# A Community
# of Crows

*Masterful mimics, inventive pranksters
or trusted friends?*

**O**N WINTER AFTERNOONS, in Framingham, Massachusetts, where Route 9 leads to Shopper's World and a McDonald's, the sky fills with the black wings of crows heading toward their winter roost. "It's like an airport there," says June Chamberlain-Auger, an ornithologist who has studied crows for the last eight years. From every direction, about an hour before sunset, crows fly in, landing one after another in long, straight lines. (A crow really does fly "as the crow flies.")

As the sun sinks, the flyways thicken to a river of black wings. Crows pour by, until the air is so choked with cawing, hurrying birds that it is almost impossible to count them. Sunset finds the grass and trees fringing the shopping center black with them. Some crows perch on the nethermost tips of nearby trees, expectant.

This winter spectacle, occurring at crow roosts across the country, has intrigued bird watchers for centuries. Recounting his vivid observations of 12,000 crows returning to their roost near Ipswich Beach, Massachusetts, in 1918, C.W. Townsend wrote he had "wished for eyes all about the head, sharpened wits and a trained assistant to take down notes."

Crows sometimes start to gather into night-roosting groups as early as August, but only as winter begins in earnest do they mass by the thousands—sometimes in tens of thousands and, occasionally, hundreds of thousands. A roost near Washington, D.C., was estimated to contain 200,000 birds. One in Rockford, Illinois, contained 328,000. A roost along the Delaware River in Pennsylvania attracted 500,000.

No one knows why crows mass like this. Various theories hold that they congregate for warmth or for protection against predators like owls or for nearby food or to exchange information. One thing is sure: the crows' reasons must be excellent, for these are uncannily intelligent birds. As the 19th-century American preacher and lecturer Henry Ward Beecher said, "Even if human beings wore wings and feathers, very few would be clever enough to be crows."

As many hunters know, crows can count. If three hunters go into a blind and only two come out, area crows know to stay away—until the third person emerges, even if it means an hour's wait. German animal trainer Otto Koehler taught his pet crows to count aloud, up to seven.

Crows can also talk. Pet crows have learned more than 100 words and up to 50 complete sentences. British ornithologist Sylvia Bruce Wilmore tells of a Staten Island crow whose owner trained him to pick pockets; if the bird found no money, he would scream, "Go to hell!" as he flew away. Crows have been known to mimic their owners' voices in order to call dogs and taunt horses.

In fact, crows will outwit almost any creature around. A crow will sometimes ride on the back of a pig foraging for mice; the minute the unwitting hog unearths its prey, the crow will steal it with a joyful chuckle. While studying crows in New Hampshire and Florida, retired virologist Lawrence Kilham saw groups of crows cooperate to raid food from otters, vultures and water birds. One technique is for a crow to pull the feasting animal's tail, distracting it long enough for another crow to make off with the booty. (Kilham observed, though, that crows will often tweak other

AS WINTER BEGINS, CROWS MASS INTO
FLOCKS NUMBERING THOUSANDS,
SOMETIMES HUNDREDS OF THOUSANDS.

animals' tails and ears for pure mischief. They like to land on sleeping cows and sheep to startle them awake; they also fly off with people's mail, pull clothespins off lines and, because they are particularly attracted to shiny objects, make off with unattended car keys.)

Crows also routinely outwit scientists. "It's really tough to work on a bird that's smarter than you are," says Donald Caccamise, a professor of biology at Rutgers University in New Brunswick, New Jersey. For the past four winters, he has been studying crows that roost at the Fresh Kills garbage dump in Staten Island.

To map their movements, he captures crows and outfits them with radiotelemetry "backpacks"—or he tries to. The problem is, he says, the crows quickly learn to recognize the university's vehicles and his equipment, because the first crows he caught warn the others. "Now we have to switch vehicles all the time and use different camouflages for the equipment," he explains.

From the 25 crows he has managed to catch and outfit, he has learned that some of the crows roosting in Staten Island commute 15 miles each morning to New Brunswick.

Cape Cod ornithologist Chamberlain-Auger, who has banded nestling crows for eight years, has found that families of crows maintain and defend feeding and nesting territories—territories they still check on daily in winter, even when food like Fresh Kills' garbage may be near the night roost.

Chamberlain-Auger and Kilham have, in separate studies, documented crows' remarkably close-knit and long-lasting family bonds. A young crow may spend up to six years with its parents before breeding on its own.

Like wolves, monkeys and people, crow families cooperate to hunt and gather, defend their territories and care for their young. That is why in the spring, you will often see three or more crows building the same nest.

Before Kilham, and then Chamberlain-Auger, published this news less than a decade ago, few people suspected that crows were capable of such tender mercies. Some people still consider crows cruel vermin—vermin because they sometimes raid crops and cruel because they will attack and kill young, weak animals.

Kilham has watched crows begin to eat dying piglets and fawns when even vultures waited with comparative courtesy. (Crows also enjoy carrion. In winter, you can sometimes see crows making off with shreds from road kills. If you follow them, you will often see the crows storing these tidbits in trees, caching the meat, like a leopard does, for later consumption. You will also see crows store nuts and seeds, sometimes burying them like squirrels, sometimes hiding them in the crevices in tree bark.)

"Crows," Kilham writes, "seem, as though by convergent evolution, to have something in their psyches corresponding to something in our own." Masterful mimics, inventive pranksters, calculating thieves, crows can also prove to be trusted friends.

When he and his wife lived in Maryland, Kilham writes, they rescued two orphaned crows. The birds often played with the Kilhams' baby in its playpen, perching on the rail. The crows watched the baby play with a silver bell on a string, until the infant let the toy go. Then a crow would seize the bell, and the baby would try to get it back.

The crows never so much as pecked at the infant, Kilham said, even when the baby grabbed at wings or tails. The birds, after all, likely considered themselves part of the Kilham family, and they were taking care of the Kilhams' infant just as they would have done for nestlings among their own family.

# Tidal Treasures

*Exploring the off-season beach*

IN WINTER, the beach becomes a different world. At first, you notice what is missing—the summer crowds, the heat, the scent of suntan oil, the cacophony of radios. The little burrowing crabs called "beach fleas" are hibernating deep in the sand. The cormorants and terns have flown south.

Now you can walk sands unscarred by human footprints, but although vacant of tan seekers, the winter beach is far from empty. Storms and migrations bring fresh wonders, a treasure trove of strange creatures and things washed up by the tide; on the East Coast, a visit to the winter beach may yield rare glimpses of snowy owls, harbor seals and sea ducks, even close looks at the world's rarest whale—none of which you could see in summer.

After a storm is a great time to visit the beach to see what the waves brought in. Along the seaweed line, you might find a sea cucumber, which is not a vegetable but an animal—a relative of the starfish that looks like a miniature football. It moves as a starfish does, by pulling itself along the ocean floor with tiny "feet"—little orange-colored sucker-tipped tubes on its underside. A lucky beachcomber may also come upon deep-sea starfish, big orange animals whose five arms are bordered with gold; or purple sun stars, starfish with 10 arms. You may spot a sea mouse, a large marine worm that looks like a hairy, headless, tailless rodent—until you turn over the six-to-eight-inch body and see the segmented golden underside.

Storms may wash up mysteries. Perhaps you will find a spiral string of flat, quarter-sized, purse-shaped "shells" that seem to be strung together. These are not shells but the eggs of the whelk snail. Inside them grow hundreds of baby snails—perfect miniatures of the eight-inch adults, complete with conchlike shells at birth. Another mystery is a single black leathery rectangle with a set of inward-curving hooks at each end. (Kids sometimes call it a "mermaid's purse.") This is the egg case of a skate, a flattened relative of sharks and stingrays.

Occasionally, a storm will bring in an unexpected harvest. Residents of Martha's Vineyard awoke one day to discover the Shellfish Fairy had come: more than 100 bushels of sweet three-inch bay scallops had been "literally blown right out of the water," said Greg Skomal, a Massachusetts state fisheries biologist who lives on the Vineyard. "It was a free-for-all for us!"

On Pacific beaches, storms may yield a harvest of jellyfish. Those most frequently washed up are the moon jellyfish and the many-ribbed hydromedusa. Alas, by the time they reach the beach, these delicate deep-water creatures, which, when floating, look like fringed Japanese lanterns, have been reduced to blobs of transparent jelly. If you see a jellyfish that sparkles like a jewel in the sun, this is a different species altogether: it is a ctenophore, whose tentacles, unlike a true jellyfish, do not sting. At night, ctenophores make the Pacific glow with natural luminescence.

Generally found floating in the tropical waters of the central Pacific, the by-the-wind sailor is another west-coast wash-up. With a body that bears growth rings like a tree, this creature resembles a cross between a sailboat and a jellyfish. The animal possesses a natural bright blue sail, which it uses to tack just like a sailboat; the rest of it is transparent. After storms, these creatures can be found piled up on the beach in windrows stretching for miles.

Seabirds, eager to forage after a day or so of waiting out bad weather, are especially active following a winter storm. You might see colorful diving ducks and acrobatic gannets, which summer farther north, overwintering at your beach. Only in winter will Cape Cod's beachgoers, for instance, spot black-and-white bufflehead ducks, goldeneye ducks, black scoters and unlikely looking red-breasted mergansers—which resemble mallards with head feathers blow-dried straight back, like characters from an episode of *The Simpsons.*

Immature loons, which breed on northern lakes, winter at sea on both the east and west coasts. On a calm day, you may hear the loon's eerie call coming from offshore.

Along the Pacific, you will be treated to sightings of red-necked grebes from Alaska's tundras and cone-bearing forests, scoters from Arctic bogs and harlequin ducks from the Yukon. All flock to Pacific shores each winter to dive for fish, snails and crabs. White-winged, black and surf scoters, which normally winter on tundra bogs, inland ponds and the Great Lakes, congregate in mixed-species "rafts" as far south as central California.

One of the most spectacular birds you might see at the beach is the snowy owl. With luxurious white-tipped plumage and a curiously catlike expression, this two-foot-tall bird of prey is often seen in broad daylight; to it, the flat, lonely expanse of the beach looks like its summer tundra home.

And from winter to early spring, you may get extraordinary views of some of North America's most endangered whales. The great, mottled forms of gray whales can be seen quite close to Pacific shores in early winter as they migrate from the Arctic to their winter breeding grounds in the bays of Baja California; in some cases, they come close enough that with binoculars, you can make out the upward curve of their mouths. These creatures were hunted to near extinction, and by the start of this century, some naturalists thought the gray whales were doomed. Today, although their numbers are growing, they are still endangered. Look for them again in the spring, when they return from Baja California—some with newborn calves.

Along the east coast, winter is the time to spot right whales. "One of the rarest mammals on Earth, and they're right here, sometimes with their bellies practically on the beach," says Stormy Mayo, director of the Center for Coastal Studies in Provincetown,

Massachusetts. These giant creatures summer in the Bay of Fundy and start showing up in New England in late December. At Provincetown, people walking along the shore have been known to glance toward the ocean to see a 50-foot whale surfacing 20 feet away.

The right whale's head looks like a huge, black rock with white barnacles on it, except that this rock moves—and opens an enormous mouth hung with baleen, comblike plates attached to the upper jaw, through which the whale strains its food. Often, people see right whales skim-feeding, mouths agape, swimming in a zigzag fashion through a patch of plankton.

It is also a thrill to spot these whales from a distance. Look for a short V-shaped spout on the horizon. ("Thar she blows!") A few humpback whales, too, may still be lingering in northern harbors before joining their comrades wintering in Bermuda. You can tell these two species apart easily, even from a distance. The right whale is the one with no back (dorsal) fin.

Eastern beaches enjoy wintertime visits from juvenile harbor seals, which migrate down from Canada and Maine, sometimes traveling as far south as Georgia. From the shore, you can watch them watching you, their black heads bobbing in the water. You will usually see harbor seals lying in big groups on rocks or on sand bars. Individuals, though, can turn up anywhere. Fishermen are occasionally alarmed to find a seal sitting in a dinghy.

Because these animals have been extensively hunted in Canada, the healthy ones are wary and will keep their distance, so bring field glasses if you want a close-up view. If you spot a disabled seal, don't try to rescue it yourself. Even baby seals have needle-sharp backward-pointing teeth, and a bite can produce a life-threatening infection. If you think a seal needs help, call the nearest aquarium.

Of course, you can never count on seeing any particular species on a given winter day at the beach. But you almost certainly will see something interesting: an exotic-looking piece of driftwood; a dead sea turtle; the shed skin of a horseshoe crab.

Naturalist Ellen Eberhardt has led winter walks for many years along the North Atlantic Coast. "Every time I go," she says, "I see something I have never seen before."

# Arctic Visitors

*The snowy owl: supreme predator*

I T BEGINS up North, as a few reports around late October: Snowy owls sighted. Sometimes it builds slowly, sometimes suddenly, with reports coming in from New England, from Minnesota. Every three to five years, around December, January and occasionally early February, what began as a flurry becomes a blizzard of snowy owl sightings—sometimes as far south as southern California and Florida.

One of the biggest years on record was the winter of 1926-27. Estimates were that 5,000 snowies were shot in the United States that winter, and observations were recorded as far south as North Carolina and West Virginia. This event—the periodic southward movement of owls en masse—is so startling, so puzzling, that it is called an irruption.

No one knows what causes so many of these big, white Arctic owls to come south. But this is not the only mystery about the snowy owl. Flying during the day—"like a huge white moth," in the words of one naturalist—the snowy is a predator of uncanny powers, with senses so sharp they seem to defy explanation.

Snowy owls appear at times and places you would least expect to see an owl. They will hunt in daylight. They don't like trees, preferring open areas instead, like beaches and fields and airport runways—flat areas that must remind them of their native tundra. They often sit on the ground, sometimes for hours.

Few birds are more exciting to see. Huge and gorgeous, standing up to 28 inches tall and weighing about five pounds, an adult female snowy is a third bigger than a great horned owl. The mostly white plumage of the adult females and youngsters is chevroned with brown, but adult males are dazzlingly snow-white.

"The most amazing thing is their eyes," says Ross Lein, a University of Calgary professor who has studied snowies for years. "These brilliant yellow eyes in this white face, surrounded by jet-black eyelids—it's spectacular. They put a stare on you like nothing else."

They are waiting for prey. Field ornithologist Simon Perkins of Massachusetts Audubon calls the snowy "the supreme predator." Most owls hunt on silent wings, surprising prey in the dark of night. Not the snowy. Hunting in the open, like a falcon, the snowy owl swoops on its prey and takes it in flight. It can muscle big Canada geese, fat raccoons, even great blue herons; yet it can also delicately snatch a tiny snow bunting.

Norm Smith, director of Blue Hills Trailside Museum in Milton, Massachusetts, has been studying snowies at Boston's Logan Airport since 1981, and still he sometimes can't believe his eyes. Once he spotted an owl across the water in Winthrop, so far away that the bird was only a speck in his binoculars. His young daughter insisted they try to trap and band the owl. To appease her, Smith baited a trap with a pigeon, even though he was sure the owl would never see it. The owl flew right to the prey.

Another time, Smith chose to use a starling as a lure to capture an owl sitting on the landing lights at the airport. A jet was taking off as Smith prepared to place the starling in the trap. The starling squawked. The owl swiveled its head. Even over the jet engines' roar, the owl had heard the starling.

Perhaps because of the snowy owl's unusual powers, Ice Age people believed it was a magical creature. In the caves at Pessac-sur-Dordogne, France, inhabited by European tundra-dwellers 20,000 years ago, anthropologists have found thousands of snowy owl claw bones. It is thought the bones were used as magic charms.

Even today, many people believe that owls possess special powers. A Native American saying holds that seeing an owl foretells a change. But what change drives the snowies south in such numbers?

For years, many naturalists believed the mass southern excursions followed a crash in the population of Arctic lemmings. (These tundra-living voles are the ones that commit suicide on cue for TV cameras. Actually, lemmings don't toss themselves over cliffs out of despair. But they do mass migrate, and if the leaders make a wrong turn—like over a cliff—the followers don't figure it out till it's too late.) When the snowies ran out of rodents, it was thought, they went south in search of other food.

The idea that lemming numbers drove owl irruptions stemmed from a 1940s paper correlating lemming numbers in Churchill, Manitoba, with snowy owl irruptions in New England. The problem with the study, Professor Lein points out, was that there are no snowy owls in Churchill.

Another theory is that bad weather might drive the birds south. During light snow years with lots of ice, there may be plenty of rodents, but the birds can't get at them very easily. Owls are known to dive through powdery snow to grab tunneling rodents, but they can't crack through crusty ice. In the winter of 1992, for example, Ottawa reported a particularly icy winter, and New England received a blizzard of snowies—40 of them in Vermont alone, the highest number ever recorded there.

Like the lemming idea, this theory casts the visiting owls as starving nomads—but in 1992, the dozens of birds Smith examined at Logan Airport were all fat and healthy. He offers a more optimistic scenario: Perhaps rather than telling of a bad winter, the owls' appearance recalls a good summer; perhaps when an unusual number of snowy owlets fledge, some must come south as "overflow." Sure enough, a high number of the owls reported during irruptions are immatures.

But no one really knows. No one even knows where in the vast Arctic they come from. The strong-winged snowy owls migrate singly and can fly enormous distances. In 1945, two snowies landed on a ship following a circular route between Gibraltar and

New York, some 1,300 miles from New York and 320 miles from Newfoundland. There are records of Asia-breeding snowies turning up as far south as Iran.

One incredibly lucky researcher was able to get reports on the whereabouts of three out of five hatchlings he had banded from one nest at Cambridge Bay, Victoria Island, British Columbia. Within a year, one was recovered along the southern Hudson Bay coast. Another was found in eastern Ontario. A third was in Siberia.

# Stories Written in Snow

## *Reading animal tracks and sign*

LONG AFTER SUNSET, the two foxes emerged from the forest to trot up the old logging road side by side. The dog fox weighed perhaps five pounds, one-third his weight when winter began; the vixen weighed only four. They were hungry.

The pair quickened their pace, picking up a scent trail. A quarter-mile away, they found the waddling 20-pound porcupine. Frenzied with hunger, they attacked its quill-less face, lunging and snapping until it was dead. And then, even though they were mates in rutting season, the dog and vixen fought over the meat. They ate everything but the tail.

All this John Kulish knew, without ever having glimpsed the individual animals involved. He read their story in the snow. "In the woods, tragedy, comedy, irony, mystery are all set down there, waiting to be read," says the octogenarian naturalist. "You don't have to be there watching the action to know what happened."

Kulish's blue eyes are clouded by cataracts, his wind-reddened ears partially deafened by age and shotgun blasts. But to him, the stories written by footprints in snow, tooth marks on bark and bubbles under ice are still as clear as print on paper, speaking as loud as the radio news.

For nearly 30 years, Kulish supported his wife and two daughters with his tracking skills, hunting and trapping in the New

England woods. The family heated its house by burning beaver-pond wood. They stuffed the freezer with venison, grouse, hare, even beaver. They paid for staples like flour and sugar with money Kulish got from otter, beaver and mink pelts and bobcat bounties. But, he says, "I never was a hunter-trapper like other people. I wasn't just interested in making money from pelts. I wanted to learn everything about these creatures. I wanted to know what makes a mink a mink, an otter an otter. I wanted to know how they thought and how they felt."

Because Kulish knows these things, he can often tell what animal left prints in a snowy field simply by looking out the window of a car speeding down a highway at 55 miles an hour. But even a neophyte tracker living in suburbia can begin to read some of the snow-scrivened dramas of the local animals. As an outdoor-education instructor at Boston University's year-round Sergeant Camp near Peterborough, New Hampshire, and at the Harris Center for Conservation Education in Hancock, New Hampshire, Kulish has taught thousands of people how.

Winter snows provide the perfect primer. We went out on a below-zero morning, when the lakes' and ponds' expanding ice cracked and boomed like thunder. ("To me, it's like a song," said Kulish. "I love it.") A light snow the night before had dusted the old ice-encrusted snow. Under these conditions, impressions of paw pads, tail drags and toenails are exquisitely clear.

Only several dozen yards from the New Hampshire state highway, along which he had parked his truck, Kulish found prints leading up an old logging road. "This," he announced, pointing to the oval four-toed prints, "is the fox trot." Even in suburbia, fox tracks are easy to find. Like domestic dogs, foxes prefer to travel along roads and paths where they know they are likely to meet other foxes. Foxes are particularly eager for company at this time of year as they search for mates. And so are skunks, opossums, raccoons and weasels.

Fox prints look like those of a terrier. In fact, said Kulish, "coyote, fox, wolf and dog all look like dog tracks." This is why it is important to look not only at the shape of the track but also at its size, depth and the pattern of the gait.

Domestic dogs, he explained, have wider chests than do their wild relatives, spreading their feet farther apart. Other ways to tell wild canids from tame: foxes, coyotes and wolves, when hunting, will place their hind feet precisely in the prints left by the forefeet. Dogs do not. And on trails that pass deep into the woods, you are not likely to find domestic dog prints without the company of human boot prints.

"When you see a track, your brain's got to tell you what the animal weighs," he said. A 35-pound coyote will sink deeper into the snow than a five-pound fox. (Later, Kulish encountered coyote tracks that had sunk six inches into the old snow. These had been made the Sunday before, a very warm day that had turned icy crust to mush.)

As the fox continued its journey, it passed several melon-sized rocks just inches from the road. These would have proved irresistible to a male fox, which would have marked them with drops of urine, like a dog does a fire hydrant. Because the fox had not marked them, Kulish knew this one was a vixen. Her periodic skid marks also told him that she was having trouble slipping on the ice under the snow, as we were.

After about a mile, the vixen chose the right fork of the logging road, and Kulish chose the left. Among the rough, thick country, steep hills and rock piles, he knew he would eventually find the round prints of a bobcat. (Which he did, but the tracks were several weeks old.)

Here, a snowshoe hare—the favorite food of the bobcat—had crossed. Many people, attempting to track a hare, will mistakenly follow it backwards, Kulish explained. Because of its gait, the prints of its larger triangular hind feet always precede the round prints of the smaller front feet. (Squirrels also have this gait, but because their toes show clearly, it is easy to see in what direction they are traveling.)

Squirrels had been out that morning, looking for food.

"Where you see a track has a lot to tell you about the creature that made it," Kulish said. Red squirrels' prints are smaller than gray squirrels', but an even easier way to identify them is by habitat: since red squirrels eat seeds and cones, their prints are found in conifer forests. Gray squirrels eat nuts and acorns and are found where oaks are more plentiful.

Kulish looks closely at trees and twigs for the stories they tell. Several weeks' snow had covered the tracks of the animal that had nibbled red maple twigs sprouting from the base of a stump, yet Kulish knew what had eaten here: "Squirrels, mice and rabbits have upper and lower incisors. If they had bitten this, it would be cut off clean, like scissors. Moose and deer are ruminants. They have incisors on the lower jaw only and gums on top."

The twigs had been roughly torn, not cleanly clipped. And nearby, four feet up its trunk, the bark of a large red maple also bore the upward-scraping tooth marks of a ruminant's lower incisors. Deer generally prefer hemlock, said Kulish. This was likely the work of moose.

Indeed, less than a mile away, Kulish spotted the big half-moon impressions of moose hooves. Because of the snow in the tracks, Kulish knew they had been made before the previous night, but still, they were fairly fresh. He judged them to be less than two weeks old. Some of the tracks were large and others small, indicating a cow moose and her yearling calf.

More moose tracks led to a badly bent yellow birch sapling. Though little more than a twig, it was raw with a curious, frantic scraping, as if someone had run a very blunt knife up and down its bark.

Less than a foot away, the answer waited in the snow. By scraping against this sapling, a 4-year-old bull moose had dislodged his loose three-pound antler, less than two weeks ago. The four-pronged antler had been cast so recently that no mice had yet gnawed it. The sculptured bone still bore the bull's hairs at the base and tiny flecks of his blood.

# Cold Facts

## *How small mammals endure winter*

O N SNOWY MORNINGS, you may wake to discover your yard crisscrossed with the trails of tiny footprints. Likely, they are the handiwork of North America's smallest mammals: mice, lesser-known shorter-tailed voles and thumb-sized pointy-nosed shrews.

Examine low-growing bushes bare of leaves. Often, even just outside cities, you will find a cuplike birds' nest roofed over with shredded material—the renovation efforts of the white-footed mouse. Look for meandering two-inch-wide paths in snow-covered meadows; these are the tunnels of voles, revealed when the surface snow has melted. And at night, if you live in the country, listen for faint whispering sounds up in the trees. The "tick" of tiny toenails hitting bark will alert you to flying squirrels landing. All these signs testify that although they seem fragile, little animals thrive despite winter's snow and cold.

In fact, these small mammals have an easier time in winter than many larger creatures. Deer, for instance, suffer immeasurably, struggling to lift their legs clear of deep snow. Big ravens and crows shiver continuously when not flying to raise their body temperature. Even the big hibernating groundhogs will be the worse for wear in winter: they emerge from their sleep looking emaciated, having lost up to one-third of their body weight. But the smallest mammals are usually still fat by winter's end, if they haven't been eaten. The tiny shrew, despite a hyperactive lifestyle, actually *gains* weight over the winter.

WEIGHING LESS THAN TWO QUARTER COINS,
A SHREW WILL FEARLESSLY ATTACK ANIMALS
MUCH LARGER THAN ITSELF.

One way to beat the cold is to huddle. In North America, 13 species of normally solitary small mammals, including the ubiquitous gray squirrel, share sleeping quarters in winter to stay warm. Cold-resistant biologists who measure such things have discovered that the temperatures in these shared nests will often be 25 degrees warmer than outside air. The underground communal nests of meadow voles may warm up to 50 degrees Fahrenheit even in January's chill. Normally solitary flying squirrels will sleep together in groups of up to 20 individuals in an elaborate nest, often in a hollow tree lined with birds' feathers and laced with grapevines.

This concentration means that if you spot signs of one flying squirrel in winter, you are likely near a mother lode. In north-country woods and fields, look for a "sitzmark," or landing spot, in an open area, with tracks leading away from it.

If these dusk- and dark-loving little animals nest near your yard, you may well attract them to your bird feeder on winter evenings. Leave the porch light on after dusk so that you can watch them glide right to the feeder.

Of course, another way animals can keep warm in winter is to come into your house. You may wake one winter morning to watch a mouse march a muffin across the kitchen counter. These rodents' caches of food are often impressive. One naturalist reported finding several gallons of seeds and nuts stored in one of his closets. (Outside, mice bury these stores one or two inches below ground.) Usually, mice remove the outer hulls of seeds and nuts before storage, presumably to save space.

The mouse's wintertime penchant for human habitation helped welcome cats into American homes. In the 1700s, reports British author and historian George Ordish, New Englanders even cut "cat holes" into the interior walls of their houses so that the felines could pursue rodents into the spaces between ceilings and floors.

If you buy a Havahart mousetrap, you can release unwanted mice outside (move the mouse at least 200 feet from your house if you don't want it to come back). If the mouse is gray with a white

belly, it is probably a sweet-smelling deer mouse or white-footed
mouse and can survive quite well outside. If the mouse is brown-
ish, it is the smellier, more destructive house mouse—not a Native
American but a European interloper that came here with the
Colonists. Most often found in cities and suburbs, this mouse, if
released, will simply find another house to move into.

Unlike mice, voles and squirrels, shrews disdain both human
habitation and the company of their own kind. Yet Joseph Merritt,
director of the Powdermill Nature Reserve in Rector, Pennsylvania,
who has studied shrews with radiotelemetry, calls the shrew "a
champion at winter survival."

Most species of North American shrews live alone. The five-
inch-long short-tailed shrew (it weighs as much as two quarter
coins, making it one of the largest of the 20 shrew species on our
continent) sleeps in an elaborately insulated grapefruit-sized nest, a
hollow ball of sedges and grasses hidden underground or under
logs, stumps or boards. By day, it probes its garden-hose-sized underground tunnels with ultrasound, using the same echolocation
ability as bats and whales. At night, the shrew emerges, leaving its
five-toed tracks in the snow. (Mice and voles, by contrast, leave
four-toed front footprints and five-toed hind prints.)

This pointy-nosed predator needs to eat its own weight each
day to fuel its hyperactive body. (The heart of the short-tailed
shrew, reports Merritt, beats 760 times a minute—10 times faster
than a human's.) A shrew will fearlessly attack animals much larger
than itself. New Hampshire naturalist Meade Cadot will never
forget the first time he saw a shrew, when he was 6 years old. The
animal was hanging by the teeth from the tip of his grandfather's
finger. "The question was whether my grandfather had caught a
shrew," Cadot remembers, "or whether a shrew had caught my
grandfather."

The shrew can afford to be fearless. It is one of the world's few
venomous mammals. Although it poses no danger to a big mam-
mal like a human, with one bite, the shrew releases a toxin that
will send a mouse into a lingering coma and immobilize insect lar-

vae for days. Thus it can keep large caches of high-calorie, high-protein prey fresh. It protects its cache by urinating and defecating on it, which makes the food unappetizing to other predators. And it has another noteworthy winter adaptation: a great capacity to generate heat from a special kind of body tissue called brown fat, which kicks into highest gear in January, when it is needed most. Taken together, the shrew's special adaptations showcase what Joseph Merritt considers "one of nature's best plans for life in the winter."

# Heaven
# Under Our Feet

*Life below the ice*

ACH WINTER MORNING while he lived at Walden Pond, Henry David Thoreau took ax and pail and went to draw drinking water from the pond. Cutting daily through a foot of snow, then a foot of ice, he would "open a window under my feet where, kneeling to drink, I look down into the quiet parlor of the fishes, pervaded by a softened light as through a window of ground glass."

It was the ice of Walden Pond that inspired one of Thoreau's most moving realizations. "Heaven," he wrote, "is under our feet as well as over our heads."

A more prosaic naturalist, however, thinking of swimming muskrat and scuttling raccoon or, for that matter, of fish and fisherman might instead offer this observation of pond ice: "One man's ceiling is another man's floor."

To the creatures that live beneath it, ice seals their watery realm off from the world above, dimming light, stilling air currents and reducing oxygen. To those that can now literally walk on the water, the frozen surface beneath their feet can serve as a tool, a trail, a toy—or a trap.

For us, the ice of the frozen pond can serve, as it did for Thoreau, as a window into lives, both above and below, that are now vastly different than in the warmer seasons.

Some pond creatures spend the winter hovering, comalike, between life and death. A carp may float motionless, embedded in a block of ice. If there is sufficient oxygen dissolved in the water, though, the fish will survive the thaw; a natural antifreeze keeps its cells from freezing and bursting. On the soft mud of pond bottoms, frogs, toads, salamanders and turtles overwinter in a sort of suspended animation, living without drawing a breath or eating a meal. The mud is always warmer than the water; a foot beneath a mantle of ice, the water temperature might be 38 degrees Fahrenheit, but four inches into the mud, it could be two degrees warmer. Although these animals don't freeze, the temperature is cold enough to slow their metabolism; they can subsist on the tiny amounts of oxygen dissolved in the water, which they absorb directly through their skin.

But all is not quiet below the ice. As Peter Marchand observes in his book *Life in the Cold,* "Maybe the hardest thing to accept about winter is that it is so alive." Sometimes, when a slow freeze creates ice free of clouding air bubbles, you can see through the ice as if through a glass-bottomed boat and watch fish swim vigorously beneath your feet. If you're very lucky, you might even glimpse a muskrat through the ice, swimming underwater with its back feet, holding its front feet under its chin and trailing a stream of pea-sized bubbles. Likely there may be mink there too, swimming beneath the ice, looking for the muskrat.

Even when the ice is thick and clouded, you can still tell much about the creatures of a pond by looking at, rather than through, its surface. Especially after a light snow, tracks and other signs of animals show up brilliantly on the ice of a pond. Water, even though frozen, is a powerful magnet for animal life.

This is one reason why Susan Morse, a forester specializing in wildlife habitat who teaches at Burlington College and the University of Vermont, leads her students to beaver ponds for her winter ecology seminars. For it is here, on the surface of the frozen pond, that you can see "the whole forest waking up and doing things and getting out and having fun."

No one is having more fun than the otters. As well as swimming beneath the ice (where they hunt for fish and probe the bottom for hibernating amphibians), they are also sliding over the slick surface, using their bellies as toboggans. (In fact, the troughs they make in the snow look so like the imprint of a child's toboggan that even Donald and Lillian Stokes were once fooled when they noticed one such trough that ran straight across a parking lot. When they saw the slide went directly into very dense underbrush, they realized what had made it.)

Cheerful daredevils, otters will use the rapids of a river—the last areas to freeze and the first to thaw—to slip under the ice. Morse has come upon their sign, incredulous: "Great chunks of ice, jags of ice sticking up like teeth, and there it is, a great big otter track. And sure enough, it disappears under the rapids"—perhaps the otter wanted to enjoy the racing water. Otters are so fun-loving that they are even known to keep playthings in their dens—stones or shells which they like to drop through the water and then chase.

Beavers have more serious business in mind this time of year. They have worked hard to make their winter livelihood possible. In a carefully built stick-and-mud lodge, a huddled family of beavers (mother, father and kits of the last two years) may enjoy temperatures up to 40 degrees warmer than the air outside. Together they have cut up to four cords of stem wood for their winter's rations, sunk with its own weight and stored in their giant underwater refrigerator.

But in spite of the beavers' best efforts, food may run out before winter's end; if so, you may see where they have slipped between the melted edges of pond ice to harvest trees and then drag them back under the ice. Though these "tree trails" obscure the beavers' tracks, there is little doubt what made them.

All this activity above, around and beneath the ice makes the pond a grocery store for predators. One winter, Morse found the evidence of a really big cat-and-mouse game: a bobcat's prints by the shore; a beaver's tree dragged into the ice; then the wide pawprints, claws out, of a 30-pound cat struggling to pull a 30-pound rodent across the ice.

To some creatures, the ice is the door to a refuge; others use ice as a trap. Hooved creatures normally avoid slippery surfaces. As Morse says, "Their feet are all wrong on the ice—it's like walking in high heels." Wolves and coyotes know this; and this is why they will sometimes drive their prey out onto the ice, as a pair of coyotes did on a pond near Morse's Jericho, Vermont, farm one winter. She read the struggle in the skift of snow atop the ice. From the prints, she could tell the deer carcass later also fed ravens, blue jays and foxes.

# Selected Bibliography

## MAMMALS

Kinkead, Eugene. *Squirrel Book.* New York: E.P. Dutton, 1980.

Lawrence, R.D. *Paddy.* New York: Ballantine, 1989.

Ryden, Hope. *Lily Pond: Four Years with a Family of Beavers.* New York: William Morrow and Co., 1989.

Shaw, William T. *The Spring and Summer Activities of the Dusty Skunk in Captivity.* Albany: The University of the State of New York, 1928.

Wishner, Lawrence. *Eastern Chipmunks: Secrets of Their Solitary Lives.* Washington, D.C.: Smithsonian Press, 1982.

## PLANTS AND FUNGI

Arora, David. *Mushrooms Demystified.* Berkeley, Ca.: Ten Speed Press, 1990.

Clute, Willard Nelson. *Our Ferns: Their Haunts, Habits and Folklore.* New York: Frederick A. Stokes Co. 1938.

Gibbons, Euell. *Stalking the Wild Asparagus.* New York: McKay, 1962.

Sterling, Dorothy. *The Story of Mosses, Ferns and Mushrooms.* New York: Doubleday 1955.

Watts, Mae Pheilgaard. *Reading the Landscape: An Adventure in Ecology.* New York: MacMillan, 1967.

## INVERTEBRATES

Evans, Howard Ensign. *Life on a Little-Known Planet.* Chigago: University of Chicago Press, 1984.

Dethier, Vincent G. *To Know a Fly.* San Francisco: McGraw, 1962.

Levi, Herbert W. and Lorna R. *Spiders & Their Kin.* New York: Golden Press, 1969.

Oldroyd, Harold. *The Natural History of Flies.* New York: W. W. Norton, 1966.

White, E.B. *Charlotte's Web.* New York: Harper and Row, 1952.

# BIRDS

Clark, Neal. *Birds on the Move: A Guide to New England's Avian Invaders.* Unity, Me.: North Country Press, 1988.

Dunne, Pete; Sibley, David; and Sutton, Clay. *Hawks in Flight.* Boston: Houghton Mifflin, 1989.

Kilham, Lawrence. *The American Crow and the Common Raven.* College Station, Tx.: Texas A & M University Press, 1989.

Voous, Karel. *Owls of the Northern Hemisphere.* Cambridge: MIT Press, 1989.

Wilmore, Sylvia Bruce. *Crows, Jays, Ravens and their Relatives.* Middlebury, Vt.: Paul Erikkson, 1977.

# GEOLOGY

Eckert, Alan W., *The Northeastern Quadrant.* New York: Harper and Row, 1987.

Little, Richard. *Dinosaurs, Dunes and Drifting Continents: A Geohistory of the Connecticut Valley.* Greenfield, Mass.: Valley Geology Publications, 1986.

# AQUATIC AND MARINE CREATURES

Carroll, David M. *The Year of the Turtle: A Natural History.* Charlotte, Vt.: Camden House Publishing, 1991.

Carson, Rachel. *The Edge of the Sea.* Boston: Houghton Mifflin, 1979.

Holling, Clancy Holling. *Pagoo.* Boston: Houghton Mifflin, 1990.

# NATURE GUIDES, FIELD GUIDES

Duensing, Edward and Millmoss, A.B. *The Backyard & Beyond.* Golden, Co.: Fulcrum, 1992.

Duensing, Edward. *Talking to Fireflies, Shrinking the Moon: A Parent's Guide to Nature Activities.* New York: NAL-Dutton, 1990.

Jorgensen, Neil. *A Sierra Club Naturalist's Guide to Southern New England.* San Francisco: Sierra Club, 1978.

Ordish, George. *The Living American House.* New York: William Morrow, 1981.

The Peterson Field Guides. Boston: Houghton Mifflin.
The Stokes Nature Guides. Boston: Little Brown.


## STORIES, ESSAYS AND EXPLICATION

Kappel-Smith, Diana. *Wintering.* Boston: Little, Brown, 1984.

Kohak, Erazim. *The Embers & the Stars: A Philosophical Inquiry Into the Moral Sense of Nature.* Chicago: University of Chicago Press, 1984.

Kulish, John. *Bobcats Before Breakfast.* Harrisburg, Pa.: Stackpole, 1969.

Marchand, Peter. *Life in the Cold: An Introduction to Winter Ecology.* Hanover, NH: University Press of New England, 1991.

Thoreau, Henry David. *Thoreau: A Week on the Concord and Merrimack Rivers; Walden; The Maine Woods; Cape Cod.* New York: Library of America, 1985.

# Index